I0024247

Ādamiyyah

I Am Therefore I Have Rights and Duties

Recep Şentürk

USŪL ACADEMY
Rooted Revival
التجديد المؤصل

First published 2025

This Usul Academy imprint is published by the registered company Usul Academy. Usul Academy is part of the Usul Foundation.
998 N Lombard Rd, Lombard, IL 60148, USA

Cover Artwork by Hatice Kübra Uyan
Cover Design and Typeset by Seda Özalkan

Usul Academy is a higher education institution established in 2021, dedicated to delivering classical Islamic sciences and contemporary subjects through a multiplex Islamic framework, with a commitment to excellence in scholarship and character.

For any queries, contact: publishing@usul.academy

ISBN: 978-1-965242-02-5

USŪL ACADEMY
Rooted Revival
التجديد المؤصل

www.usul.academy

بسم الله الرحمن الرحيم

In the name of Allah,
the Most Merciful, the Most Compassionate

About the Author

RECEP ŞENTÜRK is the Dean of the College of Islamic Studies at Hamad Bin Khalifa University, Qatar. He is also the founding president of Usul Academy. He was the founding President of Ibn Haldun University in Istanbul (2017-2021). He also heads the Adamiyya Society and the International Ibn Khaldun Society, while sitting on the editorial boards of several academic journals. He completed his PhD in sociology at Columbia University, New York. He obtained his BA in theology from Marmara University and MA in sociology from Istanbul University.

As a scholar of Islam and a sociologist, his work focuses on social theories and methods from an Islamic perspective, civilization studies, human rights, and education. Some of his notable publications include *Narrative Social Structure: Anatomy of the Hadith Transmission Network*, 610-1505 (Stanford University Press, 2005), *Comparative Theories and Methods* (Ibn Haldun University Press, 2020), *Modernization and Societal Sciences in the Muslim World* (Ibn Haldun University Press, 2021), and *Futuwwah: Noble Character* (Usul Academy, 2022). His articles on Islam and human rights, published in various academic journals and books, represent a novel approach to human dignity in Islam, based on the classical sources of Islamic jurisprudence and legal theory. Professor Şentürk's publications can be found on his website: www.recepsenturk.com.

العصمة بالآدميّة

Al-ʿiṣmah bi al-ādamiyyah

All children of Prophet Adam are entitled to the right of inviolability of life, property, religion, family, mind, and honor merely by virtue of being human.

Table *of* Contents

Preface

Our very existence, or our creation, is the foundation of our rights and duties from the *ādamiyyah* perspective. We are brought into being already endowed with rights and responsibilities. My rights are your duties, and your rights are my duties.

The Adamic Covenant (*mithāq Ādam*) signifies the primordial moral bond between humanity and God vertically, and among human beings horizontally. These bonds have been weakened, if not entirely severed, in our time. Renewing our pledge to this covenant is essential for restoring a global moral order in which justice, equality, and inviolability are upheld for all, simply by virtue of being human. We need to renew the *ādamic covenant* (*mithāq ādam*) globally if we want to move beyond the injustices we suffer today in the world.

But let me first tell you how I came across the concept of *ādamiyyah* and how it has preoccupied me since then. About twenty years ago, while reading an Arabic book on Islamic jurisprudence, I encountered this profound legal maxim for the first time: *al-ʿiṣmah bi al-ādamiyyah* (inviolability is due to humanity). The author did not innovate it, but he was reporting it from the earlier jurists who were his predecessors.

Despite having already studied theology and sociology and earned a doctorate, this was my first encounter with this concept. The book was *al-Hidāyah*, authored by Burhān al-Dīn al-Marghinānī (d. 1197), a twelfth-century Uzbek scholar. His work critically and comparatively examines Islamic law, or rather the science of *fiqh,* through evidence grounded in both reason and revelation.[1] This work is highly regarded by Muslim scholars (*ʿulamāʾ*), particularly within the Ḥanafī school, and it has been taught as an advanced textbook in seminaries (*madrasas*) from Central Asia to the Ottoman Empire, Indian Subcontinent to the Balkans for centuries.[2]

The *ādamiyyah* principle has continued to inspire me since my first encounter with it, reshaping my understanding of human rights and human dignity within the broader Islamic legal tradition. Afterward, I traveled to Egypt to learn more from the local scholars about the concept of *ādamiyyah* and its practical implications.

I met the late Tariq Bishri and explained to him the purpose of my visit. To my great surprise and disappointment, he told me, "In this land, no one knows about it. You should go back to your country and do some research about it. We will later learn it from you." This experience made me realize the urgency of reviving the forgotten concept of *ādamiyyah.*

To this end, this book reintroduces the classical concept of *ādamiyyah* and its legal ramifications in Islamic jurisprudence. While the concept of *ādamiyyah* is one of the foundational ideas of the Islamic legal tradition, its essence is not exclusively Islamic; rather, it is a shared principle across the Abrahamic faiths that signifies humanity as the fundamental common ground for all people.

This book demonstrates how this concept has been implemented for centuries across vast geographies, from India to Andalusia, as a foundation for universal human rights. I am confident that the concept of *ādamiyyah* can serve as the ground for a new world order based on new global ethics.

***

What does it mean to say that all people have rights and duties? Where do these rights come from, and on what grounds should all human beings, regardless of their race, faith, or identity, possess inherent rights? While the idea of universal human rights has enjoyed broad acceptance in public discourse since the 1948 United Nations Universal Declaration of Human Rights, it is not consistently practiced today across the globe. Moreover, basic human rights are frequently and openly violated without consequences or sanctions from the international community.

This glaring disconnect between the rhetoric of human rights and their enforcement reflects a troubling reality. Political, economic, and strategic interests override accountability, leading to clear instances of double standards, the instrumentalization of human rights, and the duplicity of authorities that leave the inhabitants of the earth unprotected under the guise of international norms, living in a state that eerily resembles the anarchy of the state of nature, where survival does not depend on rule of law but on value-free power. Much of the oppression, discrimination, racism, and injustice we witness today can be attributed to the erosion of the principled approach from the policies and practices of political bodies. This loss is significant for humanity at large.

This book presents an Islamic response to the questions surrounding the question of rights and duties by drawing from the classical literature of Islamic jurisprudence, or *fiqh*, and providing a comparative analysis of different Islamic schools of law alongside modern approaches to the issue of rights.[3] It brings to light a foundational principle in Islamic law, *al-ʿismah bi al-ādamiyyah*, that ushered centuries of peaceful coexistence among diverse communities under various Muslim states.

Throughout history, Islamic governments extended rights and protections not only to Muslims but also to non-Muslims, including followers of Abrahamic faiths such as Judaism and Christianity, as well as adherents of non-Abrahamic traditions like Zoroastrianism in Persia and Buddhism and Hinduism in India. Even the idol worshipers were granted rights and protections in Mauritania.[4] Today, the same approach may be extended to the followers of secular ideologies as they may also be considered secular religions.

Islam, from the very outset, exemplified what I call an *open civilization* by honoring the dignity of all human beings regardless of their religion, race, or culture.[5] When Prophet Muhammad ﷺ migrated from Makkah to Medina, he established a groundbreaking agreement known as *The Constitution of Medina*, which outlined the mutual rights and duties of the polytheists, Jews, and Muslims, making them equal citizens of the new state. This was the first nucleus of open civilization, which was followed by successive generations of Muslim rulers.

Why did the Prophet ﷺ and his successors adopt such an inclusive approach at a time when many other civilizations pursued exclusivity and sought to maintain their homogenous societies? What enabled Islam to establish an open civilization in contrast to its contemporaries? The answer lies in the concept of *ādamiyyah*, as I argue in this book. Grounded in the Qur'anic worldview, *ādamiyyah* provides the normative basis of Islam's political, legal, and ethical order. By centering governance and society on this principle, Islam offered a model that not only stood apart from its time but also provided a compelling blueprint for contemporary states grappling with the challenges of multiculturalism and diversity management.

Islam teaches that every human being has the right to the inviolability of life and, most importantly, freedom of religion. These rights are essential for fulfilling God's purpose in creating humanity and placing them on earth. God's purpose is to test human beings, to see how they behave, and whether they live righteously and act morally. Those who succeed in this trial earn the reward of paradise, while those who fail face consequences in the afterlife. A genuine test and trial cannot be achieved without complete freedom and inviolability. This is the existential reason why Islam upholds these rights for all human beings.

Over the past two centuries, amidst the intrusive and disruptive forces of modernization and colonialism, the Ottoman Empire remained the last government throughout the world to embrace and implement this principled approach as the basis of its social organization, state policy, and legal order. Its rights-based governance persisted from its most powerful eras, when it ruled a vast geography, until its final days in 1922.

Following the expulsion of Jews from Spain in 1492 by Ferdinand II of Aragon and Isabella I of Castile under the Alhambra Decree, many Jewish communities found refuge within Ottoman lands. Sultan Bayezid II sent the Ottoman navy to Spain to rescue the displaced Jews and Muslims, inviting them to settle in Ottoman territories. This period, beginning in the late fifteenth century, is referred to as the Jewish Golden Age under Ottoman rule. Much like their experience in Al-Andalus, Islamic Spain, these Jewish communities thrived in the Ottoman Empire, benefiting from a legal system that recognized their rights and enabled them to flourish economically, culturally, and religiously. This is one of the countless examples in Islamic history of how non-Muslims enjoyed freedom under Islamic law from the Balkans to India.

The Ottomans did not invent this universal approach to rights. They inherited it from a rich legal tradition that had been previously articulated by Ḥanafī, Mālikī, Shāfiʿī, Ḥanbalī, and the Shīʿī jurists during the formative periods of Islamic civilization. This principle was subsequently integrated into the governance of earlier Islamic states, such as the Umayyad and Abbasid Caliphate, the Mughal Empire, Andalusia, and the Seljuk Empire. Each of these states applied and adapted this legal theory, extending the protection of human dignity and rights to their diverse societies. The Ottomans further refined and institutionalized it, continuing a legacy that dated back centuries.

The concept of *ādamiyyah* asserts that all human beings, by virtue of their humanity, are endowed with inviolable rights, including life, property, religion, intellect, family, and honor. From the time of the Prophet Muhammad ﷺ through the rule of the Umayyads, Abbasids, Mughals, and Ottomans, Muslim rulers upheld this inclusive perspective, extending legal protections to people of all faiths, including Jews, Christians, Buddhists, Hindus, Zoroastrians, and Pagans.

For centuries, Islamic legal education, particularly within the Ottoman realm, centered around this universal principle, reinforcing a legal culture that safeguarded the rights of diverse communities. This framework enabled people across the Muslim world, from the Indian Subcontinent to the Balkans and Al-Andalus, to live in justice, peace, and harmony for fourteen centuries, without distinction based on school of thought, religion, race, or sex.

Yet, the concept of *ādamiyyah* has largely faded from the memory of Muslims today, as it is neither practiced nor championed by Muslim jurists or academic institutions. This is largely due to a paradigm shift and the disruption of intellectual continuity and academic independence that the Muslim world has experienced over the past century, particularly in law and political thought. Today, Muslims rely on the Western rights discourse without actively contributing to its development, expecting it to serve their needs without shaping its direction.

This book invites readers to rethink the universal concept of human dignity, rights, and duties through the lens of Islamic thought. It aspires to spark new conversations about building more inclusive and just societies while championing a vision for a just and fair world order that tackles the critical task of safeguarding basic human rights, chief among them the rights to life, freedom, and inviolability.

The hope is that this legacy will be reclaimed by Muslims and non-Muslims alike to address the pressing human rights challenges and unprecedented crises we face today. Reviving the *ādamiyyah* principle, which holds that the dignity and inviolability of all human beings are inherent and universal, is essential for any pursuit of establishing open civilizations.

By rekindling an awareness about the *ādamiyyah* principle, this work aspires to inspire renewed perspectives that would open pathways toward a more just and peaceful world for all.

***

The book concludes with a call for an *Ādamiyyah* covenant, bringing together all human beings to establish a global order where justice, equality, and freedom prevail. The *Ādamiyyah* covenant could be the ideal common ground for humanity to create a new global ethics and legal framework. This would represent a 'third generation' of human rights, addressing and remedying the existing shortcomings in current human rights laws and practices. It is an extension of my earlier research on the concept of *ādamiyyah* and human rights. I have drawn from my previous works to shape this current volume.

I thank the Center for Islamic Studies (İSAM), where I first encountered the concept of *ādamiyyah*. I am also grateful to Abdullahi An-Naim for facilitating my semester at Emory University Law School, which allowed me to advance my research on *ādamiyyah* and human rights. The British Academy Fellowship provided me with the opportunity to present and discuss my work with colleagues at Oxford Brookes University and other universities across the United Kingdom, which helped me greatly refine my research.

I also thank my colleagues at Doshisha University in Japan for inviting me to present my findings and for their valuable feedback. I would like to extend my sincere gratitude to the Pontifical Institute for Arabic and Islamic Studies (PISAI) and its President, Diego Sarrió Cucarella, for inviting me to present the idea of *ādamiyyah* in Rome, as well as to Stephen B. Young, Global Executive Director of the Caux Round Table for Moral Capitalism, and Ibrahim Zain for their contributions. I am grateful to my friends in the Adamiyya Society who share and promote the same vision. I also thank Jeroen Harun Vlug, Pakeezah Saadat, and Abdulrahman Alsanad for their contributions. My special thanks to Seda Özalkan for her passionate dedication to excellence while editing, proofreading, and designing this book.

Recep Şentürk

Notes

1. Al-Mārghinānī was an authoritative Islamic jurist and legal scholar who played a major role in the consolidation, systematization, and elaboration of the Ḥanafī school of jurisprudence. His book represents the pinnacle of Islamic legal training, preparing Muslim scholars for careers in the Islamic legal administration of the Islamic polity. For an English translation, see Burhān al-Dīn al-Farghānī al-Marghinānī, *Al-Hidāya: The Guidance*, Vol. 1, trans. Imran Ahsan Khan Nyazee (Bristol: Amal Press, 2006).
2. In contemporary times, the term *madrasa* has acquired a negative connotation associated with cultural stagnation and radicalization. However, historically, the *madrasa* was an esteemed institution of higher learning, serving as a precursor to the contemporary university. It played a central role in advancing scholarship in fields such as medicine, geometry, law, philosophy, and the natural sciences. For a detailed analysis of how the Islamic *madrasa* influenced the development of Western education systems, including the rise of colleges and universities, see George Makdisi's *The Rise of Colleges: Institutions of Learning in Islam and the West* (Edinburgh: Edinburgh University Press, 1981). Additionally, for an in-depth overview of the classical *madrasa* curriculum, which was designed to cultivate well-rounded scholars, refer to Hamza Karamali's *The Madrasa Curriculum in Context* (Abu Dhabi, UAE: Kalam Research and Media, 2017).
3. There is an ongoing debate surrounding the use of the term "Islamic law" to describe what is referred to as *fiqh* within the indigenous Islamic legal tradition. I have explored this topic in depth in my other works. For the purposes of this book, it suffices to note that the classical *fiqh* tradition encompasses far more than what is currently understood as "law" in the Western legal context, including areas such as morality and ethics. Nonetheless, for the sake of clarity and accessibility, I use the terms "Islamic law" and "Islamic jurisprudence" throughout this work. The same clarification applies to the use of "Islamic legal scholar" and "Muslim jurist" as translations for *faqīh*.

4. Tareq Sharawi, "How Does Islam Treat People Outside the Abrahamic Religions? Between Ādamiyyah and Ibrāhimiyyah," PhD diss. (Ibn Haldun University, 2020), and of the same author, "The Inviolability of the Non-Muslims in Islamic Law: A Comparative Reading of Modern and Classical Debates," *Afkār: Journal of 'Aqidah and Islamic Thought* 1 (2020): 79-112.
5. See my article "Unity in Multiplexity: Islam as an Open Civilization," *Journal of the Interdisciplinary Study of Monotheistic Religions* 7 (2011): 49-60.

Introduction

Throughout my travels in the Muslim world, I have met, talked to, and even eaten with people who in America would have considered 'white'— but the 'white' attitude was removed from their minds by the religion of Islam. I have never before seen sincere and true brotherhood practiced by all colors together, irrespective of their color.

—Malcolm X (El-Hajj Malik El-Shabazz), *Letter from Mecca,* 1964

From the window of my high school in Istanbul's Fatih district, I could see a world that embodied centuries of peaceful coexistence. To my left stood the Orthodox Patriarch's Church in Fener. Across the Golden Horn was the Chief Rabbi's Synagogue in Karaköy. And overlooking it all was the Caliph's Palace in Topkapı. Three monuments, three faiths, all visible from one window. I often found myself asking: How could they coexist side by side in a world where differences so often sow discord? What was the secret to their harmony?

The answer, I would later discover, lay deep within the foundational principles of Islam, principles that had guided multi-ethnic, multi-religious states, nurtured cultures, and cultivated what I now call *open civilization.*[1] At the heart of this openness was the concept of *ādamiyyah,* the dignity of humanity, not confined to creed or color, but inherent in every person simply by being human. This principle, which shaped governance and society under Islamic rule, was established long before the emergence of universal human rights discourse in seventeenth-century Europe.

Nonetheless, the purpose here is not to frame the discussion on rights as a contest of historical precedence but rather to highlight how various religious and legal traditions, including Islam, Christianity, and Judaism, in their authentic forms, converge on core values and principles that affirm human dignity and the universality of rights. Islam, in particular, presents itself as an authentic continuation and culmination of the same divine message conveyed to Prophet Moses and Jesus, peace be upon them, originating from the same divine source and perfected in its final form.

However, while these earlier traditions deviated from their original teachings, Islam restored this shared theological, moral, and legal framework, reaffirming the universal principles of human dignity and justice. By grounding rights in the intrinsic value of humanity itself, rather than specific religious or ethnic identities, Islam offers not just a parallel to these earlier traditions but a reclaimed and revived path toward an inclusive and universal framework for peaceful coexistence on earth.

The historical experience of Islamic civilization is rich with examples of this openness. From its emergence in the seventh century, Islam embraced an inclusive approach to the civilizations it encountered, extending protection not only to Abrahamic people, who had a special status in Islamic law, such as Jews and Christians, but also to non-Abrahamic communities, like Zoroastrians, Hindus, and Buddhists. From the Prophet's covenants with the Christians of Najrān, the Monks of Mount Sinai, and the Jews of Medina to the multi-ethnic societies of Andalusia, Mughal India, and the Ottoman Empire, Islamic governance demonstrated a striking inclusivity.[2]

This openness was institutionalized in what became known as the *millet* system, a multi-civilizational social and political structure where different faith communities, or *millet*s, governed their internal affairs while coexisting peacefully under Islamic rule. This book argues that the secret behind this unparalleled historical experience of coexistence lay in the concept of *ādamiyyah,* a recognition of the inherent dignity of all people.

Human Rights: A Western Concept?

Fundamental human rights have been integral to all legal frameworks grounded in divine revelation throughout history. Religions, particularly Abrahamic traditions, share common values and principles regarding human inviolability. As such, the Muslim jurists did not promote Islamic exceptionalism or claim superiority for being the originator of human rights. Instead, these principles are seen as the universal foundation for the legal frameworks of these religions. The aim of this book, then, is not to argue that Islam pioneered the concept of universal human rights ahead of the West but to highlight that religions, in their authentic forms, and traditional legal systems, commonly share a version of human rights grounded in similar universal values and norms.

Nevertheless, many people who have received a Eurocentric education may think that the concept of human rights is exclusively a Western construct, expressive of Enlightenment values developed out of the European experience. This assumption hinges on the belief that human rights emerged solely from Western legal and moral traditions and that no such idea exists in Islamic thought.

However, the classical texts of Islamic jurisprudence reveal the opposite. Far from being a foreign concept, universal human rights, grounded in the principle of *ādamiyyah* (the inherent dignity of all human beings), have been an essential part of Islamic legal and ethical thought for centuries, predating much of modern Western human rights discourse.

The concepts of human rights (*ḥuqūq al-ādamiyyīn*) and the inviolability of human beings (*ʿiṣmah al-ādamiyyīn*) are well-established principles within the Islamic legal tradition. Likewise, other foundational concepts, such as axiomatic principles (*kulliyyāt*) and the essential objectives of law (*ḍarūriyyāt al-khamsah* or *maqāṣid al-sharīʿah*), which are rooted in the Qur'anic worldview and early Islamic jurisprudential texts, further illustrate the centrality and essentiality of human rights in the formation of Islamic thought and civilization.

Thus, while Islam embraces the concept of inherent and universal human rights, the distinctive nature of its legal framework lies not merely in affirming these rights. The distinctive characteristic of human rights from an Islamic perspective rests in the philosophical foundations and the underlying reasoning used to justify why such rights should be granted. Specifically, the question of "Why do all people have rights?" receives different answers across various religions, ideologies, and civilizations, and it is in these justifications that the divergence between Islam and other worldviews becomes evident. This will be further elaborated in Chapter 4, where I delve into the philosophical foundations that underpin the Islamic approach to human dignity and rights.

Hope or Threat? What Islam Has to Offer to the World

Islam is arguably the fastest-growing religion in the world today, which raises questions and concerns for Western societies that have growing Muslim populations. If Muslims were to become a majority community one day, how would they treat their neighbors? What would they contribute and what would they have to offer to Western societies?[3]

These questions rightfully worry local populations, and as Islam spreads, the public discourse tends to become dominated by answers from security experts, journalists, and politicians who have little or no grounding in Islam. In this climate, Muslims carry the burden of proof, especially given the relentless anti-Muslim propaganda with widespread misconceptions and stereotypes about Islam, fueling public fear and creating adversity between Muslims and their neighbors.

Moreover, the impact of colonialism, the ideology of the "white man's burden," and the imposition of Western modernity have estranged many Muslims from Islam's intellectual, political, and moral heritage, severing them from the very foundations of their tradition. This rupture has disrupted the transmission of knowledge across generations and weakened the continuity of Islamic thought and governance.

As a result, it has become increasingly challenging to articulate Islam's enduring contributions to contemporary societies. Reconnecting with this legacy is essential, not as an intellectual exercise, but as a means to revive the principles that can guide communities toward justice, social harmony, and the common good.

As we shall see, the Islamic tradition and its political history and jurisprudence address these worries. In Islamic law, all human beings possess inviolability, regardless of their creed, color, class, or culture. The classical books of Islamic jurisprudence and the history of Muslim rule extending from India to the Balkans testify, conceptually and practically, to the inviolability of all human beings in Islam. Moral, legal, and political theories in Islam, as well as state practices over vast geographies across centuries, assure us that Muslims, if grounded in their tradition, would bring glad tidings to today's societies.

A powerful example of how these ideals can impact contemporary struggles is found in the transformative journey of Malcolm X.[4] A prominent African American civil rights leader, Malcolm X's pilgrimage to Makkah in 1964 profoundly altered his outlook on race and human equality. In Makkah, he encountered a fraternity unlike anything he had known, a sacred space where people of all colors and backgrounds stood side by side for worship, united as equals before God.

This experience shattered his previous notions about race and led him to conclude that Islam's principles of human dignity and brotherhood offer solutions to the racial and social divisions still haunting the West. His experience in Makkah demonstrated that equality and fraternity are not abstract ideals but lived realities. This is a powerful cue that the growing presence of Muslims in the West is not a cause for fear but an opportunity, one that invites societies to rethink coexistence through the principle of shared humanity.

Malcolm X's Letter From Mecca to America

April 20, 1964

Never have I witnessed such sincere hospitality and the overwhelming spirit of true brotherhood as practiced by people of all colors and races here in this Ancient Holy Land, the home of Abraham, Muhammad and all other prophets of the Holy Scriptures. For the past week, I have been utterly speechless and spellbound by the graciousness I see displayed all around me by people of all colors.

I have been blessed to visit the Holy City of Mecca. I have made my seven circuits around the Ka'ba, led by a young Mutawaf named Muhammad. I drank water from the well of Zem Zem. I ran seven times back and forth between the hills of Mt. Al-Safa and Al-Marwah. I have prayed in the ancient city of Mina, and I have prayed on Mt. Arafat. There were tens of thousands of pilgrims, from all over the world. They were of all colors, from blue-eyed blonds to black skin Africans. But we were all participating in the same rituals, displaying a spirit of unity and brotherhood that my experiences in America had led me to believe never could exist between the white and non-white. America needs to understand Islam, because this is the one religion that erases from its society the race problem.

Throughout my travels in the Muslim world, I have met, talked to, and even eaten with people who in America would have considered 'white'— but the 'white' attitude was removed from their minds by the religion of Islam. I have never before seen sincere and true brotherhood practiced by all colors together, irrespective of their color.

You may be shocked by these words coming from me. But on this pilgrimage, what I have seen, and experienced, has forced me to re-arrange much of my thought patterns previously held, and to toss aside some of my previous conclusions. This was not too difficult for me.

Despite my firm convictions, I have always been a man who tries to face facts, and to accept the reality of life as new experiences and new knowledge unfolds it. I have always kept an open mind, which is necessary to the flexibility that must go hand in hand with every form of intelligent search for truth.

During the past eleven days here in the Muslim world, I have eaten from the same plate, drunk from the same glass, and slept in the same bed, (or on the same rug)—while praying to the same God—with fellow Muslims, whose eyes were the bluest of blue, whose hair was the blondest of blond, and whose skin was the whitest of white. And in the same words and in the actions and in the deeds of the 'white' Muslims, I felt the same sincerity that I felt among the black African Muslims of Nigeria, Sudan and Ghana.

We were truly all the same (brothers)—because their belief in one God had removed the 'white' from their minds, the 'white' from their behavior, and the 'white' from their attitude. I could see from this, that perhaps if white Americans could accept the Oneness of God, then perhaps, too, they could accept in reality the Oneness of Man—and cease to measure, and hinder, and harm others in terms of their differences in color. With racism plaguing America like an incurable cancer, the so-called 'Christian' white American heart should be more receptive to a proven solution to such a destructive problem.

Perhaps it could be in time to save America from imminent disaster—the same destruction brought upon Germany by racism that eventually destroyed the Germans themselves. Each hour here in the Holy Land enables me to have greater spiritual insights into what is happening in America between black and white. The American Negro never can be blamed for his racial animosities—he is only reacting to four hundred years of conscious racism of the American whites.

But as racism leads America up the suicide path, I do believe, from the experience that I have had with them, that the whites of the younger generation, in the colleges and universities, will see the handwriting on the wall and many of them will turn to the spiritual path of truth—the only way left to America to ward off the disaster that racism inevitably must lead to. Never have I been so highly honored. Never have I been made to feel more humble and unworthy. Who would believe the blessings that have been heaped upon an American Negro?

A few nights ago, a man who would be called in America a 'white' man, a United Nations diplomat, an ambassador, a companion of kings, gave me his hotel suite, his bed. By this man, His Excellency Prince Faisal who rules this Holy Land, was made aware of my presence here in Jedda. The very next morning, Prince Faisal's son, in person, informed me that by the will and decree of his esteemed father, I was to be a State Guest. The deputy Chief of Protocol himself took me before the Hajj Court. His Holiness Sheikh Muhammad Harkon himself okayed my visit to Mecca. His Holiness gave me two books on Islam, with his personal seal and autograph, and he told me that he prayed that I would be a successful preacher of Islam in America.

A car, a driver, and a guide, have been placed at my disposal, making it possible for me to travel about this Holy Land almost at will. The government provides air-conditioned quarters and servants in each city that I visit.

Never would I have even thought of dreaming that I would ever be a recipient of such honors—honors that in America would be bestowed upon a King—not a Negro. All praise is due to Allah, the Lord of all the Worlds.

Sincerely,

El-Hajj Malik El-Shabazz
(Malcolm X)

The Divine Design of Diversity

In the contemporary world, the unprecedented increase in geographic mobility has led to a remarkable rise in social diversity across societies. People from different cultural, ethnic, and religious backgrounds now coexist more closely than ever before. Some perceive it as a threat to their homogeneous identities and seek to suppress, exclude, or even eradicate those they deem different. History and present realities alike attest to the devastating consequences of such exclusionary ideologies. From ethnic cleansing and forced assimilation to systemic discrimination and genocide, such ideologies have repeatedly been wielded as instruments of erasing diversity.

Yet, from an Islamic perspective, diversity is neither an accident of history nor an anomaly but a fundamental aspect of the divine order. According to the Islamic vision of society, diversity is a God-given condition. The Qur'an affirms that human differences, whether in language, ethnicity, or culture, are a manifestation of God's will: "*O mankind, indeed We have created you from male and female and made you peoples and tribes so that you may know one another. Indeed, the most honored of you in the sight of Allah is the most righteous of you. Indeed, Allah is All-Knowing, All-Aware.*" (Qur'an 49:13)

This verse tells us that diversity is not a source of conflict but a means for mutual recognition. It also emphasizes that human worth is not contingent upon race, lineage, or nationality but is instead dependent on righteousness and moral integrity. Islam, therefore, does not conceive of humanity as a monolithic entity but as a constellation of distinct societies and individuals, bound together by a common foundation, our humanity (*ādamiyyah*).

Thus, no human effort can eliminate diversity.[5] Attempts to impose uniformity are not only futile but also defy the very nature of creation. Every being is a unique manifestation of the divine, for God's creation never repeats itself. The challenge, therefore, is not to suppress diversity but to build a social order that acknowledges and upholds the dignity of all people.

Yet, despite the divine wisdom in human plurality, modern and postmodern ideologies have sought to reconstruct human identity based on arbitrary standards that inevitably lead to suffering and discord. In their pursuit of ideological conformity, they overlook the natural diversity inherent in creation by neglecting human nature and divine will. These efforts, driven by the desire to enforce a singular, artificial notion of identity, ultimately fail because they contradict the fundamental reality of human diversity. Only by embracing the plurality that God has ordained can humanity move toward a future where coexistence is not merely tolerated but valued as an essential part of human civilization.

The Architecture of Islamic Fraternity

The Islamic approach to managing diversity is grounded in the laws of fraternity (*ḥuqūq al-ukhuwwah*), which operate on four interconnected levels: (1) fraternity in creation (*makhlūqiyyah*), (2) fraternity in humanity (*Ādamiyyah*), (3) fraternity in the Abrahamic faiths (*Ibrāhīmiyyah*), and (4) fraternity of the Muslim community (*Muḥammadiyyah*).

At the most universal level is fraternity in creation (*makhlūqiyyah*), which emphasizes the interconnectedness of everything that exists: humans, animals, plants, and the physical world.

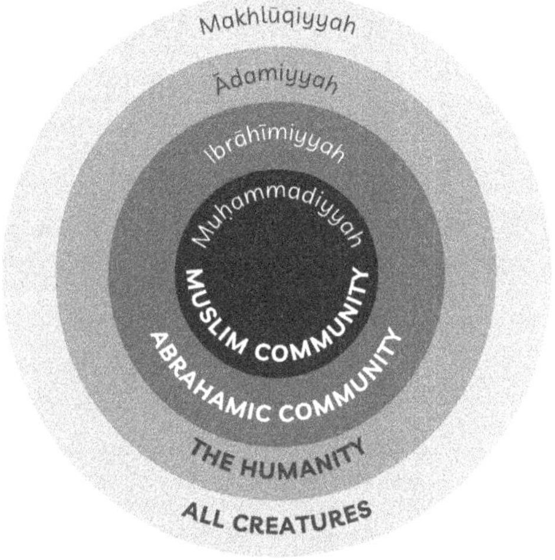

Figure 1. Levels of Fraternity

All creation shares a common origin from the same divine source, the Creator (*al-Khāliq*), and embodies the attribute of being created. This common condition of createdness establishes an ethical foundation that obliges humans to care for all forms of life. All that exists is a sign (*āyah*) of God's wisdom and power, pointing toward its Maker.[6] This perspective is of paramount importance in cultivating an ethical disposition toward the environment and all forms of life.

The second tier is the fraternity in *Ādamiyyah*, which highlights the universal bond among all human beings through their shared descent from Adam (peace be upon him), the first human and messenger of God who was sent down from paradise to earth. This level of brotherhood transcends distinctions of race, ethnicity, and religion and affirms a universal brotherhood grounded in the idea that all humans originate from the same earthly substance, referred to as "brotherhood in clay" (*al-ukhuwwah fi al-ṭīn*). As beings created from soil, all humans are inherently equal in their essence and dignity.

Fraternity in *Ibrāhīmiyyah* forms the next tier and accentuates the bonds between Jews, Christians, and Muslims. These communities share a common spiritual ancestry, tracing their faith traditions to Prophet Abraham (peace be upon him), the father of all monotheistic prophets. This shared heritage reflects common principles of faith, law, and morality that unite the followers of these religions.

Lastly, the fraternity in *Muḥammadiyyah* acknowledges Prophet Muhammad ﷺ as the exemplar and guide of the *ummah*, the global Muslim community. The Qur'an proclaims that all believers are brothers and sisters and that the criteria for nobility and superiority are determined by *taqwā,* God-consciousness, piety, integrity, and virtue. In addition, Prophet Muhammad's ﷺ *ummah* consists of two groups: those who have already embraced his call (Muslims) and those who are still invited to join the faith (the rest of humanity).

This model not only acknowledges diversity as a natural and divine reality but also emphasizes the moral and ethical responsibilities that accompany it. Through these interconnected layers of fraternity, Islam encourages individuals and societies to transcend differences and act with kindness and responsibility toward all creation.

In an increasingly fragmented world, the consequences of neglecting these responsibilities are evident at all levels, from the degradation of the environment to the erosion of human relationships. Islam's vision of interconnectedness offers a blueprint for addressing these crises by promoting harmony between humanity and the natural world, as well as between individuals and communities.

Ādamiyyah: *The Law of Universal Brotherhood and Sisterhood*

Muslims have historically approached their fellow humans with a spirit of fraternity, viewing them as either brothers and sisters in *Ādamiyyah* or *Ibrāhīmiyyah.* As expressed above, the Islamic principle of *ādamiyyah* acknowledges the inherent dignity and rights of all children of Adam. This idea is expressed through key Arabic concepts that form the essence of divinely ordained rights: *ʿiṣmah al-ādamiyyīn* (the inviolability of human beings), *ḥurmah al-ādamiyyīn* (the sanctity of human life), and *karāmah al-ādamiyyīn* (the dignity and honor owed to every person).

Throughout history, these principles have guided the governance and legal systems of Islamic civilization, where diversity was managed through an understanding of fraternity at the levels of *Ādamiyyah*, *Ibrāhīmiyyah*, and *Muḥammadiyyah.* At its height, Islamic civilization flourished on this inclusive vision and established an open civilization that accommodated vast cultural, ethnic, and religious diversity. Their legal system safeguarded the rights and protections of diverse religious communities and ethnic minorities.

The result was a remarkable degree of social harmony, wherein numerous ethnicities, religions, and languages coexisted peacefully. This pluralistic order enabled diverse communities to participate fully in economic, intellectual, and cultural life while preserving their distinct identities. Several historians have noted that if Muslims had intended to eradicate other cultures and religious communities, they had the power to do so, but history tells a different story. Unlike many empires that sought to enforce religious uniformity through forced conversions, systematic persecution, or mass

Muslim rulers chose policies that allowed diverse faiths and cultures to coexist peacefully. English educator and historian Thomas W. Arnold (1864–1930) observed:

> "Of any organized attempt to force the acceptance of Islam on the non-Muslim population, or of any systematic persecution intended to stamp out the Christian religion, we hear nothing. Had the caliphs chosen to adopt either of these courses, they might have swept away Christianity as easily as Ferdinand and Isabella drove Islam out of Spain, or Louis XIV made Protestantism penal in France, or the Jews were kept out of England for 350 years. The Eastern Churches in Asia were entirely cut off from communion with the rest of Christendom, through-out which no one would have lifted a finger to help them, and their position was more helpless than that of any other Christian community in the world. The survival of these churches to the present day is a strong proof of the generally tolerant attitude of the Muhammadan governments towards them."[7]

Had it not been for the fundamental principle of *ādamiyyah* in Islam that upholds the inherent dignity of all human beings and the state's duty to protect them, Muslims possessed the power to impose their rule and could have eradicated the diverse cultures under their governance. If their objective had been the destruction of other civilizations, as some historians suggest, the nations, religions, and languages that predate the Arab conquests would not have survived to this day. Yet, history proves otherwise. The continued existence of these communities serves as undeniable evidence that Islamic governance, rather than seeking to erase diversity, created conditions that allowed various cultures and faiths to survive and, in many cases, thrive.

However, in modern times, the rise of exclusionary ideologies has eclipsed the principle of *ādamiyyah*, which resulted in the marginalization of human dignity as a universal value. Today, there is an urgent need to revive Islam's legacy of an open civilization, grounded in the principle of *ādamiyyah,* as a means to promote peace and justice globally. This revival demands a deliberate effort to reengage with classical Islamic frameworks, particularly those concerning human rights (*ḥuqūq al-ādamiyyīn*). This revival would not only restore Islam's rich heritage but also provide essential tools to address contemporary challenges of pluralism and diversity.

Notes

1. See my article "Unity in Multiplexity: Islam as an Open Civilization," *Journal of the Interdisciplinary Study of Monotheistic Religions* 7 (2011): 49-60.
2. For a detailed analysis of Prophet Muhammad's Covenants, see Ahmed El-Wakil and Ibrahim Mohamed Zein, T*he Covenants of the Prophet Muhammad From Shared Historical Memory to Peaceful Co-existence*, Routledge Studies in Islamic Philosophy (London: Routledge, 2022).
3. This part incorporates and adapts ideas from my earlier work, Recep Şentürk, "Islamic Law and the Children of Adam," *Renovatio: The Journal of Zaytuna College*, Vol. 6, No. 1 (2022).
4. See Şentürk, Recep. *Malcolm X: The Struggle for Human Rights (*Claritas Books, 2019).
5. This idea can be found in the Qur'an in Surah al-Māʾidah (5:48): "*We have revealed to you O Prophet this Book with the truth, as a confirmation of previous Scriptures and a supreme authority on them. So judge between them by what Allah has revealed, and do not follow their desires over the truth that has come to you. To each of you We have ordained a code of law and a way of life. If Allah had willed, He would have made you one community, but His Will is to test you with what He has given each of you. So compete with one another in doing good. To Allah you will all return, then He will inform you of the truth regarding your differences.*"
6. See Şentürk, Recep. *Semiotics of Nature: Recharging Nature with Meaning for Environmental Ethics and Action.* (2025) Forthcoming.
7. Thomas Walker Arnold. *The Preaching of Islam: A History of the Propagation of the Muslim Faith,* 2nd ed. (London: Constable & Company, 1913), 79.

CHAPTER ONE

Human Rights: A Sociological Analysis

"Do not let the enmity of any people provoke you to deviate from justice."

—The Qur'an, *Sūrah al-Mā'idah* 8

The question of whether human rights are a product of Western civilization or a universal concept transcending cultural boundaries lies at the heart of many debates in human rights discourse. Is the idea of human rights an invention of the Enlightenment, uniquely Western in origin, or does it reflect values and principles that have existed across diverse civilizations throughout history? This inquiry leads us to explore two dominant perspectives: the Eurocentric evolutionist approach and the universalist approach. The former views human rights as an outcome of Western experience, and the latter sees them as universal, originating from the common values of all human traditions.

The Eurocentric evolutionist view claims that human rights are a unique product of Western civilization. According to this view, non-Western civilizations, including Islamic, Indian, Chinese, and African cultures, lack human rights frameworks because they represent earlier, less-developed stages of human evolution. However, this narrative has faced significant criticism for disregarding the existence and sophistication of human rights discourse within other civilizations and legal traditions.[1]

This perspective forms the foundation of Orientalist thought, which portrays the West as the cradle of freedom and progress while casting the East as a cradle of despotism. The main project of the Orientalist perspective is to legitimize Western colonialism under the guise of a civilizing mission.[2] Scholars like Jack Donnelly, Ann Elizabeth Mayer, Abdullah an-Naʿim, and Bassam Tibi support variations of this approach.[3]

Conversely, the universalist approach argues that the notion of human rights is not exclusive to Western culture but is a universal phenomenon present in various forms across all civilizations. Proponents of this view reject the idea that human rights discourse is a Western construct. Muslim scholars who advocate for a universalist understanding of human rights argue that Islam, from its emergence, recognized and enshrined the dignity of all individuals. While the Eurocentric approach often aims to dismiss the presence of human rights in Islam, the universalist perspective seeks to draw on Islamic principles to enrich contemporary human rights discourse.

There is a valid critique of human rights discourse that argues it is often wielded as a tool of Western imperialism, reflecting Western hypocrisy, particularly concerning the rights of Muslims. While this critique holds truth, it should not lead to a wholesale rejection of the concept of human rights. Some critics, especially within radical circles, argue that Islam has nothing to do with human rights due to this perceived hypocrisy. Paradoxically, this view aligns with pro-Western modernist claims that human rights have no roots in Islamic thought.

John Locke and Natural Rights

Within the Eurocentric framework, human rights are commonly understood as deriving from the natural rights tradition pioneered by John Locke (1632-1704), a foundational thinker in Western political thought. This perspective frames the development of human rights as an evolutionary process, tracing their progression from Ancient Greece through Roman and Medieval times, the Renaissance, the French Revolution, and culminating in the establishment of the United Nations. While earlier traditions, such as Roman law, medieval Scholasticism (e.g., Thomas Aquinas), and the *Magna Carta*, included elements of rights-based thinking, these frameworks were limited in scope, focusing on specific social classes or contexts, and lacked a universal, systematic articulation of natural rights inherent to all human beings.

Locke, however, is credited with providing a cohesive philosophical articulation of natural rights that directly influenced later human rights discourse. His articulation of natural rights to *life*, *liberty*, and *property* is widely regarded as the foundation of contemporary human rights theories and practices.[4] These rights, entitlements held by virtue of being human, are considered natural because their source is human nature itself, rather than societal constructs or government decrees. Locke's philosophy significantly influenced key historical documents, including the Declaration of Independence and the U.S. Constitution, by embedding the ideals of natural rights into the foundation of modern democracy.

Even after Locke's modern articulation of universal human rights, the implementation of these principles did not materialize immediately but gradually over time: initially limiting them to specific segments of society, such as property-owning men, before extending them to include men without property and, eventually, women. A clear example of this is the expansion of the right to vote and be elected in Western societies throughout history. Although the US is an important cradle for the human rights discourse, Afro-Americans living in the country were able to obtain human rights only recently after long-standing struggles. And still, many problems persist today that arise from the practice of discrimination.

Similarly, the status of Native Americans is still ambiguous. Even though a universal perspective on human rights existed in the authentic versions of Abrahamic religions, as will be discussed below, Locke's philosophy marks a departure from earlier Western discourses on human rights, which were predominantly exclusivist.

This raises an intriguing question: how did Locke develop his inclusive ideas? Interestingly, Locke knew Arabic and attended lectures by Edward Pococke, the first Professor of Arabic Studies at Oxford.[5] It is plausible that these lectures included more than just language instruction, delving into Arabic literature, history, and civilization, including the legal and political theories of the Islamic world. Such exposure suggests that Locke might have encountered Islamic ideas on governance and the relationship between the ruler and the ruled.

C. G. Weeramantry similarly contends that Islamic jurisprudence was one of the sources of Western legal and political thought, and both Locke's and Rousseau's thinking, especially their theories of sovereignty, could well have been influenced by Islamic thinking on the relationship between subjects and the state.[6] This potential intellectual exchange points to the interconnectedness of civilizations in the development of the philosophy and theory of rights, challenging the Eurocentric narrative that frames its evolution as an exclusively Western development.

As will be explored further, the inclusive character of Islamic law's rights framework, established from the outset, stands in contrast to the Western trajectory, which took centuries to achieve broader inclusivity. Comte Léon Ostrorog, in a lecture delivered at the University of London post-World War I, highlighted this significant distinction.[7] He remarked that Islamic legal principles, developed by Eastern thinkers of the ninth century, included profound doctrines of justice and human rights. He noted: "*...they expounded a doctrine of toleration of non-Muslim creeds so liberal that our West had to wait a thousand years before seeing equivalent principles adopted.*"[8]

"Life, Liberty, and Property"

A contemporary proponent of the Eurocentric perspective, or anyone who regards Locke as the founding father of natural rights discourse, might be surprised to encounter the principles of life, liberty, and property articulated in the works of Muslim jurists like Al-Dabūsī (d. 1039 CE) and Al-Sarakhsī (d. 1090 CE). Their writings, foundational to Ḥanafī jurisprudence, predate the Magna Carta by two centuries and Locke's treatises on natural rights by more than half a millennium.

Human rights theorizing in Islamic civilization traces its roots not only to the works of jurists like Al-Dabūsī but also to earlier Muslim scholars and the Qur'an itself. The example of Al-Dabūsī's work alone is sufficient to expose the weakness of Eurocentric arguments that claim human rights as an exclusively Western construct or seek the origins of universal human rights conceptualization solely within Western traditions. From the seventh to the eleventh century, Islamic jurists had already systematized human rights in ways that surpassed the sophistication of many modern doctrines.

As seen in the excerpt below, these jurists explicitly state that all human beings (*ādamī*) are endowed with *ʿismah* (inviolability), *hurriyyah* (liberty), and *milkiyyah* (ownership)—the very same triad articulated by Locke as life, liberty, and property.[9] In the remaining part of this chapter, we will trace the genealogy of human rights, exploring their development and articulation across Islamic and other traditions.

God-Given Universal Rights to Life, Liberty, and Property*

Al-Dabūsī (d. 1039 CE), *Taqwīm al-Adilla fī Uṣūl al-Fiqh*

فالله تعالى لما خلق الإنسان لحمل أمانته أكرمه بالعقل والذمة حتى صار بها أهلا لوجوب الحقوق له وعليه فثبت له حق **العصمة والحرية والمالكية** بأن حمله حقوقه وثبت عليه حقوق الله تعالى التي سماها أمانة ما شاء كما إذا عاهدنا الكفار وأعطيناهم الذمة يثبت لهم حقوق المسلمين وعليهم في الدنيا. والآدمي لا يخلق إلا وله هذا العهد والذمة فلا يخلق إلا وهو أهل لوجوب حقوق الشرع عليه كما لا يخلق إلا وهو حر مالك لحقوقه وإنما يثبت له هذا الكرامات بناء على الذمة وحمله حقوق الله تعالى.

When God the Almighty created humanity to bear His trust, He honored them with intellect and legal capacity, making them inherently eligible to carry rights and responsibilities. Thus, God granted humans the right to **inviolability**, **liberty**, and **ownership**, enabling them to fulfill their entrusted duties. Alongside these rights, God also imposed obligations upon humanity toward Him, which He referred to as trust, according to His will. Just as when we made a covenant with non-Muslims and granted them protection, the rights and duties of Muslims in this world are extended to them, a human being is created inherently endowed with this covenant and legal capacity. Every human is created eligible to bear the responsibility of religious-legal obligations placed upon them, just as every human is created free and possessing ownership of their rights. This dignity is conferred upon them based on their legal capacity and their role in bearing the divine trust assigned to them by God the Almighty.

*Al-Dabūsī, Abū Zayd ʿAbd Allāh ibn ʿUmar. *Taqwīm al-Adilla fī Uṣūl al-Fiqh*. Edited by Khalīl Muḥyī al-Dīn al-Mays. (Beirut: Dār al-Kutub al-ʿIlmiyyah, 2001), p. 417.

The Abrahamic Origins of Human Rights

All heavenly religions initially had a God-given law that promoted fundamental rights and freedoms. However, they were unable to preserve the foundation of faith and law due to corruption during the historical process. As a result, religious doctrines and laws lost their universal and divine character. Instead, they adopted a more localized character that made distinctions based on faith, class, race, and sex.

Nevertheless, this observation may not apply to all adherents of the pre-Islamic religions in question. In fact, the Qur'an distinguishes between the People of the Book *(ahl al-kitāb)* who did and did not participate in the corruption by saying, *"But they are not all alike. There are some among the People of the Book who are upright, who recite God's revelations during the night, who bow down in worship."* (The Qur'an 3: 113) From this, we understand that even if the dominant discourse in pre-Islamic religions shifted away from universal rights principles, certain groups remained committed to defending these values. For example, within Judaic tradition, the commandment to "love your neighbor as yourself" (Leviticus 19:18) has been interpreted from two perspectives.

One interpretation is a particularistic or exclusivist perspective, which limits the term neighbor (*re'a*) to fellow Jews as seen in the *Mishneh Torah*. The other is a universal perspective, where the term neighbor (*re'a*) is extended to all humans. For instance, Ben Azzai argues that this verse implies the sanctity of every human being, not just Israelites, as all are created in the image of God (Genesis 5:1). Nehama Leibowitz, a 20th century Biblical scholar, also refutes the idea that "neighbor" in the context of loving others should be limited to Jews, as the term is used in Exodus 11:2 to refer to Egyptians.[10]

While the legal frameworks before Islam grappled with both exclusivist and universal interpretations, the prevalent view was the exclusivist perspective that restricted rights to members of specific religious or ethnic groups. In these legal systems, people were regarded as the property and slaves of kings, and the law was seen as the command of kings. During wartime, no principles were recognized, and civilizations were destroyed. People were discriminated against based on race, religion, language, sex, wealth, and lineage.

Until recent times, both Jews and Christians recognized the inviolability of the members of their faith communities exclusively, and even this recognition was limited. Their theological and legal interpretations did not typically accommodate pluralistic social structures, as seen in their histories as well as in contemporary societies. Even the rights of members of their own religion could be violated by religious and political authorities. On the other hand, Christian and Jewish communities coexisted and thrived in the Islamic world from the seventh to fifteenth centuries, coinciding with what is referred to in Eurocentric historiography as the Middle Ages, and beyond, while Muslim or Jewish communities in Christian Europe were not granted similar protections and rights until the advent of secularism.[11]

This disparity in treatment can be traced back, in part, to some theological misinterpretations within these traditions. For instance, some Jews believed that they were a chosen community and that God was exclusively the God of the Jewish people; thus, non-Jews had no dignity. This belief fundamentally contradicts the universal concept of human rights. Christianity emerged, so to speak, in contradistinction to such exclusivism, promoting a message of universal love.

However, as Christianity became widespread, its original message became entangled with political agendas, which resulted in deviations from its foundational principles of inclusivity. This resulted in the marginalization of non-Christians and, at times, denying their right to life.

This exclusionary stance contributed to a long history of discrimination, not only against non-Christians but also against women within Christian communities. Particularly notable was the inequality between men and women, where Christian legal and social norms often placed women in subordinate roles. The eventual legal equality of men and women in many Christian societies was the result of protracted struggles and gradual reform rather than an inherent aspect of Christian doctrine.

Nonetheless, it would be inaccurate to generalize all Jews and Christians under one view regarding human rights, as diverse interpretations have existed throughout history. As a matter of fact, many Christian theologians, interpreting biblical teachings, advocate for the inherent freedom and dignity of all people, defending universal human rights as aligned with Christian values of justice, equality, and love for humanity.

Human Rights in Pre-Islamic Arabia

Before Prophet Muhammad ﷺ, the law of the prophets Abraham and Ismail had been corrupted, and the concepts of human dignity and inviolability were largely absent in the Arabian Peninsula during the Period of Ignorance (*jāhiliyyah*). In this era, human life, property, and rights were primarily protected within tribal affiliations, with no protections for foreigners or slaves.

Nonetheless, the remnants of the concept of universal rights in pre-Islamic Arabia can be seen in the practice of the Sacred Months (*al-ashhur al-ḥurum*), during which the inviolability of individuals extended beyond tribal boundaries, offering protection to all, albeit within a limited scope. Anyone seeking refuge in the Kaʿbah was considered inviolable. The concept of inviolability existed in the pre-Islamic Arab society, though it was restricted to specific times, places, or people. Islam universalized this notion and extended the sanctity and protection of life, property, and dignity to all people, at all times and places.

Human Rights and Prophet Muhammad ﷺ

Human rights in Islam originate directly from its theological foundation: the divine revelation given to Prophet Muhammad ﷺ. In contrast to the gradual evolution of human rights in the West, which developed through struggles and concessions against oppressive political authorities, human rights in Islam emerged naturally from its core theological principles.

From the outset, human dignity and human rights in Islam were divinely ordained and further affirmed through the practices and teachings of Prophet Muhammad ﷺ. These principles are centered on the ultimate sovereignty of God and the divinely endowed inherent dignity (*karāmah*) of all human beings, as stated in the verse, "*Indeed, We have dignified the children of Adam.*" (Qur'an, 17: 70) As such, the principles of justice, dignity, and inviolability were not developed in response to societal demands but rather revealed as foundational elements of the faith, meant to be upheld across time and place.

The rights set forth in the Qur'an and embodied in the Prophet's actions are as relevant today as they were at their inception. Thus, human rights in Islam have not undergone the kind of evolutionary process seen in the West. The rights that existed at the beginning continue until today.

As mentioned earlier, the pre-Islamic *jāhiliyyah* period was marked by numerous injustices. In response to these injustices, a group of noble individuals in Makkah formed the *Ḥilf al-Fuḍūl* (League of the Virtuous) in order to defend justice and protect human rights. Prophet Muhammad ﷺ was also among the members of this group. Even before receiving revelation, Prophet Muhammad ﷺ exemplified a profound respect for human dignity. He advocated for the fair treatment of all people, including slaves, women, orphans, and non-Muslim communities that were marginalized or mistreated in pre-Islamic Arabia. He ﷺ instructed his followers to treat servants and laborers with kindness and challenged the exploitative norms of the time. His interactions with non-Muslims were likewise marked by great esteem. He visited the sick regardless of their faith and ensured that captured prisoners were treated humanely.

Prophet Muhammad ﷺ and a Jewish Rabbi

A Lesson in Human Rights

« مَنَعَنِي رَبِّي أَنْ أَظْلِمَ مُعَاهِدًا وَغَيْرَهُ »

A Jewish rabbi once came to the Prophet ﷺ to demand payment on a debt the Prophet owed him. The Prophet ﷺ said to him, “O Jew, I currently have nothing to give you.” The Jewish rabbi responded, “Then I will not leave you, O Muhammad, until you pay me.” The Prophet ﷺ replied, “I shall sit with you, then,” and did so. The Prophet ﷺ prayed the noon, afternoon, sunset, final evening and morning prayers, and his companions were threatening and menacing the man, the Prophet ﷺ being aware of what they were doing. They then said, “O the messenger of God, is a Jew keeping you in restraint?[1]” to which the Prophet ﷺ replied, “My Lord has prevented me from wrongdoing anyone under a covenant, or anyone else.”

When the day came to an end, the Jewish rabbi, observing the Prophet’s patience, said, “I bear witness that there is no god but Allah and that you are indeed the Messenger of Allah. Half of my wealth is for the sake of Allah. I swear by God that my only purpose in treating you as I have done was that I might test the description of you given in the Torah: Muhammad, son of Abdullah, born in Makkah, who would migrate to Taiba, and whose kingdom is in Syria, a man of unmatched gentleness, neither harsh nor rude, not given to shouting in the marketplaces or to vulgar speech. I bear witness that you are indeed the Messenger of Allah, and here is my wealth. Use it as Allah wills.”

This *ḥadīth* is reported by Al-Bayhaqī in *Dalāʾil al-Nubuwwah* (The Signs of Prophethood).

From the earliest revelations in Makkah, the Qur'an emphasized justice, mercy, and the sanctity of life. It addressed the rights of the vulnerable, including orphans, the poor, and slaves, and condemned injustices prevalent in pre-Islamic society, such as usury, exploitation, and tribal violence. These verses called for social reform and reminded the early Muslim community that every human being possesses inherent dignity bestowed by God.

The Prophet's respect for human dignity extended to everyday interactions. On one occasion, as a Jewish funeral procession passed in front of the Prophet ﷺ, he stood up. When someone remarked that it was the coffin of a Jew, the Prophet ﷺ replied, "*Is he not a human*?" (*a laysat nafsan*). These actions established a precedent for human rights in Islam. Prophet Muhammad ﷺ lived and taught a message of human dignity, justice, and universal rights that permeated every aspect of his leadership and life.

The Constitution of Medina

When the Prophet ﷺ and his companions migrated to Medina from Makkah, he took immediate steps to build a community where people of different faiths could live together peacefully. *The Covenant of Medina*, which he established, was an unprecedented legal agreement that guaranteed safety and religious freedom for everyone in the city, including Muslims, Jews, and polytheists. It was one of the first written agreements that placed all groups under the same rights and responsibilities, effectively making them equal citizens within the newly formed community. He condemned tribal chauvinism and reminded his companions that no person held superiority over another except by virtue of piety and righteousness.

In his farewell sermon, Prophet Muhammad ﷺ proclaimed just as the times of pilgrimage are inviolable, so are all times, and just as the Sanctuary of Makkah is sacred, all places are inviolable. He extended this inviolability (*ḥurmah*) to all people, affirming the sanctity of their life, property, and honor. Some scholars view the *Covenant of Medina* as the first written constitution and the *Farewell Sermon* as the first human rights declaration. These foundational legal documents granted rights to all people by virtue of their humanity.

The Prophet's example was like a seed that took root and flourished over centuries. Ultimately, a pluralistic society, legal system, and political structure emerged in Islamic territories that accommodated non-Muslims from various religious communities. While pluralism in other parts of the world developed in spite of prevailing religious systems, in Muslim lands, this pluralistic framework developed as a direct outcome of the inherent inclusivity of Islamic law.

Living Well Together: Muslim Spain, Mughal India, and the Ottoman State

As Islamic governance expanded under various caliphates and dynasties, from the Umayyads and Abbasids to Al-Andalus, Mughal India, Persia, and the Ottoman Empire, it developed a distinctive model of inclusive society. Throughout history, Muslim states established governance structures that upheld religious freedom and protected the rights of minority communities. Their inclusive administrative systems ensured stability and contributed to economic prosperity and intellectual development.

Not only did Abrahamic communities, such as Jews and Christians, but also non-Abrahamic communities, such as Hindus, Jains, and Buddhists, coexisted peacefully under Islamic rule. This pluralism precipitated remarkable cultural and architectural achievements, including the construction of landmarks such as the Qutub Minar, the Taj Mahal, and Fatehpur Sikri. These experiences demonstrate the flexibility of Islamic governance in addressing diverse social contexts to create vibrant and peaceful societies, even in settings where Abrahamic faiths were not predominant.

One of the most renowned examples of coexistence was *la convivencia*, a term used to describe the pluralistic society of Muslim Spain (Al-Andalus), which thrived for nearly seven hundred years, from 711 to 1492. Al-Andalus, the region of the Iberian Peninsula under Islamic rule, stands out as an extraordinary model of governance marked by an unparalleled degree of multiculturalism and intellectual flourishing. As we will explore in later chapters, the foundation of this historical experience of peaceful coexistence stemmed from the Islamic legal principles concerning dignity.

This theoretical legal framework translated into a justice system in practice, which established multiple jurisdictions to safeguard the rights and autonomy of diverse religious and ethnic groups vis-à-vis the political authority of the state.

This inclusive environment, where minority communities enjoyed religious freedom, legal autonomy, and socio-political protection, provided a fertile ground for intellectual flourishing. Scholars from different faiths collaborated, exchanged ideas, and enriched various fields of knowledge. In Al-Andalus, Jewish philosophers like Solomon ibn Gabirol (1021–1058), Samuel ibn Naghrillah (993–1055), and Maimonides (Mūsā Ibn Maymūn) (1135–1204) thrived alongside their Muslim counterparts, including Ibn Ṭufayl (1110–1185) and Ibn Rushd (1126–1198). Their engagement with Islamic philosophy enhanced Jewish intellectual traditions, with figures like Maimonides integrating Islamic Aristotelianism into Jewish thought. This intellectual exchange across cultural and religious boundaries in Muslim Spain spurred advancements in philosophy, science, medicine, and the arts. This experience left a lasting legacy of cross-cultural collaboration that influenced both the Islamic world and later European thought and the Renaissance.

Similarly, Mughal India (1526–1857) demonstrated the ability of Islamic governance to adapt to a highly diverse and multi-religious society in predominantly non-Abrahamic religious landscapes. The Indian context required engagement with non-Abrahamic people. Islamic governments, including the Delhi Sultanate and the Mughal Empire, adopted policies that ensured their religious freedom and social autonomy within the framework of Islamic governance.

The Ottoman Empire (1299–1922) likewise exemplified an inclusive model of governance through its *millet system*, which granted religious minorities, Jews, Christians, and others, a high degree of legal and cultural autonomy. Under this system, each religious community had the right to govern its own affairs, including marriage, education, and internal legal disputes, under the oversight of its own religious leaders. This inclusive legacy reached its most formalized expression during the Ottoman Empire in what came to be known as the *millet* system. This legal and social arrangement provided structured autonomy for non-Muslim communities, allowing them to govern their own religious and legal affairs while simultaneously facilitating their inclusion within the broader Islamic polity.

These efforts to institutionalize the protection of human rights as an official state policy reached their most formalized expression in the Ottoman Empire through the Tanzimat reforms (1839-1876) (*ıslahat fermanları*), several international treaties, and the establishment of a constitutional framework. The Ottoman reforms integrated the principles of human dignity and inviolability into the modern legal and constitutional structure of the empire. Islamic law, supplemented by legal codes (*qānūnnāmah*) and royal edicts (*farmān*), played a crucial role in shaping this transformation.

Such an evaluation suggests that these legal developments represent a continuity in Islamic law, albeit adapted to align with the evolving political and administrative structures of the time, rather than a radical departure from its foundational principles. The reforms introduced during the Tanzimat era and subsequent constitutional movements can thus be seen as an extension of the long-standing tradition of legal pluralism and administrative flexibility within Islamic governance. However, this continuity was framed in a new discourse that engaged with the demands of modernization, international diplomacy, and emerging notions of statehood.

Yet, scholars like Wael Hallaq challenge this interpretation and argue that modernization introduced fundamental disruptions. According to this view, the adoption of Western legal frameworks, particularly the codification of laws, centralized state control, and the shift away from juristic interpretation (*ijtihād*) and local judicial autonomy, marked a significant departure from the authentic practice of Islamic law leading to a legal system that is neither fully Islamic nor entirely Western.[12] As a result, the modernization of Islamic legal systems is seen by some scholars as a rupture that fundamentally altered the way law functioned within Muslim societies.

This debate raises critical questions about the nature of continuity and change in Islamic legal traditions: Was the Tanzimat and constitutional reform period a pragmatic adaptation of Islamic governance to modern realities, or did it represent a fundamental rupture that distanced Islamic law from its classical roots? The answer largely depends on one's perspective. Those who view these reforms as an extension of Islamic legal flexibility emphasize the structural adjustments that enabled Islamic principles to persist within a changing political and legal landscape. In contrast, others argue that the paradigmatic shifts introduced by modernization, such as the adoption of codified laws, the erosion of juristic pluralism, and the increasing dominance of state-controlled legal institutions, redefined the very nature of

Islamic law by altering its epistemological and methodological foundations, sources of authority, and mechanisms of interpretation.

Mechanisms for Human Rights Jurisdiction

As previously discussed, human rights in Islam did not emerge in opposition to state authority but were rather implemented and safeguarded through it. The application of Islamic legal principles of justice and human rights across different contexts, such as al-Andalus, India, and the Ottoman state, cannot be fully grasped without an in-depth understanding of the Islamic governance paradigm, which differs significantly from the modern nation-state model.

The Islamic governance paradigm is built upon a distinctive conception of sovereignty and legal authority that enables the application of Islamic legal and ethical principles across diverse social contexts. Its institutional framework, in which governance is bound by the rule of law rather than the arbitrary will of rulers, functions as a stabilizing mechanism that ensures the application of the foundational principles despite changes in political leadership. As a result, universal principles remain intact as the system allows for adaptation to changing circumstances and prevents these principles from being undermined by the shifting priorities of successive rulers.

According to Islamic law, every social relationship and behavior carries a legal or moral normative value (*ḥukm*) which is an essential aspect of human action (*ʿamal*). According to Sunnis, this normative value is a divinely assigned qualification of action and is subject to contextual variations, whereas the Muʿtazilah views it as an essential or inherent property of the action itself. However, both schools agree that humans do not create these values but rather uncover them, either through pure reason or divine guidance. Consequently, identifying normative values in events and relationships and acting accordingly is the personal duty of every responsible Muslim (*mukallaf*). The state or administrators cannot make decisions at this point on behalf of individuals.

In modern social systems, moral judgments are determined by those in positions of power. Social organizations establish ethical norms within their hierarchical structures, and individuals are expected to conform. Delegating moral judgment to the powerful has been framed as a disciplinary necessity that legitimizes the exclusion of subordinated individuals from active moral reasoning and decision-making. By contrast, Islamic law regards moral judgment as a natural, non-transferable right and duty of every individual. The diversity of scholarly opinions on legal norms is a natural consequence of this principle, as disagreements in interpretation arise from the freedom to engage in legal reasoning.

Modern legal systems, however, require standardized moral and ethical frameworks to ensure stability and predictability. Positive law is the clearest manifestation of this drive toward standardization. In Islamic jurisprudence, legal norms (*aḥkām*) are preordained by Allah rather than being subject to the will of rulers. The will of the ruler is valid to the extent that it coincides with the already imposed divine legal norm on that specific issue. In this context, the ruler's opinion holds no greater epistemic weight than that of any other individual in the quest to uncover normative truth.

Nevertheless, the ruler's legal preference is binding to maintain order, as governance would be untenable without authoritative decision-making. However, in cases where individuals lack sufficient knowledge to interpret and apply legal verdicts, this function is carried out by expert legal scholars (*mujtahidūn*), who are themselves civil individuals, not representatives of an authoritarian institution akin to a state-controlled church.

Regarding legislative structures, continental European legal systems historically centralized legislative authority within the state, whereas the Anglo-Saxon tradition preserved a greater role for local customs in the formation and functioning of law. In cases where the state holds exclusive legislative power, mechanisms are necessary to prevent governmental overreach and protect fundamental rights and freedoms. In contrast, Islamic legal traditions balanced state authority with decentralized legal scholarship through a nomocratic governance paradigm where law derived its legitimacy from divine principles rather than state-imposed norms.

The inherent rights and liberties bestowed upon humans by God at birth can be discerned through divine revelation or reason. In Islamic governance, the primary duty of the state is not to legislate but to apply and uphold the law.[13] Unlike the modern nation-state system, where legislation is the exclusive function of the government, Islamic governance traditionally does not monopolize the legislative process.

Historically, legislation in Islam was largely a civil endeavor carried out by religious scholars (*ʿulamāʾ*), except during the era of the Rightly Guided Caliphs. These early caliphs exercised legal interpretation (*ijtihād*) because they were either legal experts (*mujtahids*) themselves or relied on the collective scholarly consensus (*ijmāʿ*) and the majority opinion (*jumhūr*) of the companions. However, their legal authority was not derived from their political position but from their scholarly qualifications. As Islamic governance evolved, caliphs who lacked the expertise to make independent legal rulings deferred to scholars, who maintained legal authority independently of the state.

This distinction between state power and legal authority is a defining feature of Islam's nomocratic system, in which governance is bound by the rule of law rather than the arbitrary will of rulers. The Qur'an and Sunnah are the constitutional foundations of Islamic law, and the state has no authority to alter or revoke these principles. Instead, its role is limited to implementing the law by adopting one of the legal interpretations developed by qualified jurists (*mujtahidūn*).

This nomocratic approach remained intact even during the modernization period, as demonstrated by the codification of Islamic legal principles in the *Mecelle* (*Majallah al-Aḥkām al-ʿAdliyyah*), the nineteenth-century Ottoman legal code that integrated Islamic jurisprudence into a structured legal framework that preserved the juristic foundations of Islamic law while adapting to administrative reforms.

State Authority vs. Individual Rights

In Islamic governance, the state traditionally stands outside the process of law formation, and it cannot arbitrarily override individual rights through excessive use of power. As a result, Islamic legal tradition does not exhibit the same structural tension between individual rights and state authority that has historically shaped human rights discourse in the West. Whereas Western legal traditions have largely framed human rights as a safeguard against state encroachment, Islamic law, when legislation remains within the domain of scholars (*ʿulamāʾ*), does not necessitate such a conflict.

However, when the state assumes the role of legislator, as has occurred in modern Islamic societies influenced by Western legal models, it becomes imperative to establish clear limits on state legislative authority to prevent government overreach and safeguard fundamental rights and liberties. In recent times, this concern has become increasingly urgent as legislation in much of the Islamic world has deviated from its traditional scholarly foundations and has instead become a centralized function of the state.

As modern nation-states monopolize legislation, a critical question arises: To what extent do these laws align with the universal principles of Islamic law? This remains a matter of significant debate, as the centralization of legislative authority challenges the decentralized, scholar-led legal tradition that historically characterized Islamic governance.

Nomocracy and the Limits of Political Authority

In Islamic civilization, political authority is constrained by divine law. The power of the state leader and administrators is not absolute but operates within the framework of the *Sharīʿah*, which stands above all temporal authority. No ruler or government has the right to override the universal principles established by Allah and the Prophet ﷺ in the Qur'an and Sunnah.

Unlike systems where sovereignty is vested in the state, Islamic governance follows a nomocratic model, in which the legitimacy of political authority is derived from adherence to divine law. The state, even in its executive capacity, is not the source of religious authority, nor do the individuals exist to serve the state. Instead, the state exists to serve the welfare of individuals, whose ultimate accountability is to God alone.

This foundational principle is succinctly captured in the maxim, "*There is no obedience to the creation in disobedience to the Creator.*"[14] In essence, obedience to human authority is conditional upon its alignment with divine law. The Qurʾan and Sunnah define the boundaries of legitimate governance and ensure that political power, which is a divine trust (*amānah*) in its original purpose, does not devolve into an instrument of oppression.

By upholding this principle, Islamic governance historically sought to prevent despotism and reinforce justice as the central objective of political authority. The parameters stipulated by the sacred texts (*naṣṣ*) define the limits of political authority and determine the extent of an individual's obligation to obey rulers. However, obedience to authority is not without limits either.

According to Islamic law, rulers, including the head of state, may only demand obedience in matters that are good (*ma'rūf*). Any demand for obedience in matters that are prohibited or unjust (*munkar*) is considered illegitimate, regardless of who issues the order. In such cases, those subjected to injustice not only have the right to disobey but are, in fact, obliged to enjoin what is right and forbid what is wrong.

Majid Khadduri calls such a system of administration "nomocracy," a legal and political order in which the supreme authority rests with divinely ordained laws.[15] In the Islamic tradition, nomocracy refers to a system where governance is bound by divine law rather than political expediency. These principles, known as *al-ḍarūriyyāt al-kulliyyāt al-shar'iyyah,* the essential, universal objectives of Islamic law, are drawn from the Qur'an, *Ḥadīth*, and the consensus (*ijmā'*) of scholars. These rules are immutable and apply to all people at all times. Neither religious scholars (*'ulamā'*) nor rulers (*umarā'*) can alter them.

The defining feature of nomocracy is the permanence of legal rulings derived from the Qur'an and Sunnah. These principles are immutable, meaning no legislative body, including scholars or rulers, has the authority to alter them. This distinguishes Islamic nomocracy from modern legal systems, where laws are subject to change based on political will and shifting societal interests. Unlike modern states, where legislative, executive, and judicial powers are monopolized by the state, nomocracy distributes these powers to prevent the concentration of power that leads to tyranny. In this system, scholars (*ulamā'*) are responsible for interpreting and deriving legal rulings based on *Sharī'ah*, while statesmen (*umarā'*) are tasked with executing and enforcing these laws. On the other hand, the state as an executive entity has restricted legislative authority, confined to *ta'zīr* (discretionary punishments for offenses not explicitly defined in *Sharī'ah*). It cannot enact laws that contradict divine principles. This separation between legal and political authority creates a system of checks and balances and prevents rulers from exerting absolute control over the legal and moral foundations of society.

In a nomocratic system, the protection of fundamental human rights is not an arbitrary state policy but an intrinsic feature of governance. Rights such as life, property, religion, family, and freedom of expression are enshrined in divine law, which renders them inalienable and beyond the arbitrary reach of the state.

For instance, the state cannot take a life or confiscate property without a lawful justification, as both are protected under divine law. Religious freedom is safeguarded, ensuring that no individual can be coerced into conversion or compelled to follow a particular interpretation of Islam. Family life is protected, meaning the state cannot arbitrarily dissolve marriages or separate children from their parents. Likewise, the honor and dignity of individuals are inalienable rights that prevent the state from humiliating, oppressing, or unjustly dishonoring its citizens.

If the state fails to uphold these fundamental rights, it loses its legitimacy within Islamic governance. Moreover, if the state itself becomes an oppressor, violating the very principles it is bound to uphold, resisting or opposing such a government is not only lawful but a moral obligation, as it no longer represents legitimate authority under *Sharī'ah*.

Nomocracy versus Rule of Law

While nomocracy and the modern rule of law share the idea that no one is above the law, they differ fundamentally in the source and nature of legal authority. In nomocracy, laws are derived from divine revelation and are unchangeable, whereas in democratic systems, laws are crafted by legislative bodies and are subject to modification based on the political will of the majority. In a democratic rule-of-law system, laws evolve with society and reflect majority rule, while in a nomocracy, fundamental legal principles remain fixed beyond the reach of temporal authority.

This contrast is especially relevant today, as many Muslim-majority countries operate under secular legal frameworks where state-driven legislation holds ultimate authority. Nomocracy, by contrast, offers an alternative model in which the state does not wield absolute legislative power but instead, by its very nature, curbs the centralization of authority. In contrast to Schmittian notions of the "state of exception," where sovereignty is defined by the ability to suspend the law, nomocracy leaves no room for such suspensions, as the divine legal framework remains binding in all circumstances to prevent rulers from exploiting crises to expand their power.[16] This nomocratic system developed long before similar concepts took shape in Europe, where the idea of limited political authority evolved gradually over centuries, influenced by milestones such as the Magna Carta, Enlightenment thought, and later constitutional developments.

Another key distinction between the rule of law in secular systems and Islamic nomocracy lies in its approach to legal authority and application. Nomocracy is not defined by rigid, unchanging laws but is instead founded on permanent and inviolable principles. However, its application remains casuistic: legal rulings are adapted to specific cases rather than imposed as a fixed statutory code detached from real-world contexts. Unlike modern legal frameworks, which rely on positive law that can be amended or repealed, nomocracy operates within a jurisprudential tradition that maintains permanent divine principles while allowing for legal adaptability through scholarly reasoning and interpretation.

In this system, the scholars (*ʿulamāʾ*) are, in reality, the interpreters of the law, not its legislators. Their role is to derive legal rulings through *ijtihād*, the legal reasoning that considers context, precedent, and evolving circumstances while remaining anchored in divine law. This is the meaning of the principle that ultimate sovereignty belongs to Allah, not human institutions or political authorities. Through *ijtihād*, legal decisions are tailored to the diverse individual cases in order to warrant that justice is applied contextually rather than through standardized codification.

Changing Contexts, Lasting Values: Ijtihād

Although the fundamental principles of *sharīʿah* remain immutable, their practical application evolves in response to shifting social, cultural, and historical circumstances. This is where *ijtihād,* or independent legal reasoning, plays a pivotal role. The *ulamāʾ* bear the responsibility of interpreting how divine principles apply across diverse contexts, taking into account changes in economic, social, and political conditions. However, *ijtihād* operates within strict parameters. It must align with the primary sources of *sharīʿah,* the Qur'an, Sunnah, and consensus of scholars, and cannot override explicit scriptural commands. In this way, Islamic law, through *ijtihād*, evolves alongside society without straying from its fundamental principles.

The Epistemology of Ẓanniyyāt

A fundamental characteristic of Islamic legal thought is its epistemological approach to the levels of certainty in knowledge. Islamic legal discourse distinguishes between *ẓannī* (non-definitive) and *qaṭʿī* (definitive) rulings, and the vast majority of legal rulings fall into the *ẓannī* category. This classification is based on two factors: *thubūt* (authenticity) and *dalālah* (meaning). The first category concerns whether a legal text is definitive in authenticity (*qaṭʿī al-thubūt*), such as the Qurʾan and *mutawātir ḥadīth*, or non-definitive in authenticity (*ẓannī al-thubūt*), such as *āḥād* reports in *ḥadīth*. The second category pertains to whether the meaning of a text is clear and unambiguous (*qaṭʿī al-dalālah*) or open to multiple interpretations (*ẓannī al-dalālah*).

Since many legal texts are either *ẓannī* in their authenticity or indication, *ijtihād* becomes necessary to extrapolate legal rulings. Each qualified scholar can arrive at valid interpretations of Islamic law, meaning that no single ruling holds absolute authority over others. Legal validity does not stem from claims to absolute truth or institutional power but rather from the rigorous and consistent application of legal principles (*uṣūl al-fiqh*). Since the majority of Islamic legal rulings fall under *ẓannīyyāt*, no single scholar or institution holds a monopoly over absolute truth in jurisprudence. Ultimate normative truth belongs to Allah alone, and scholars engage in *ijtihād* as a means of approximating divine will rather than asserting definitive rulings in most legal matters.

This epistemological humility has historically promoted legal pluralism. Multiple valid interpretations exist within the Sunnī legal traditions reflected in the existence of four Sunnī schools of thought (Ḥanafī, Mālikī, Shāfiʿī, Ḥanbalī) as well as the Shīʿī traditions. This decentralized structure also ensures that no political or religious institution can claim an exclusive right to define normative truth. Because legal rulings remain interpretative rather than absolute, Islamic governance does not allow for centralized legal authoritarianism and prevents any political or religious institution from monopolizing the law. Thus, no single scholar or school dictates the law for the entire Muslim community. Instead, multiple juristic opinions coexist, creating a legal framework that allows for adaptability and flexibility while maintaining continuity with Islamic legal tradition.

This epistemological foundation upholds legal diversity while also reflecting the humility of human interpretation in the pursuit of divine guidance. By embracing interpretative plurality, Islamic nomocracy stands apart from secular legal systems, which derive legitimacy from human authority, and rigid theocratic models, which centralize religious interpretation within a single institutional framework.

Human Rights as an Independent Discipline

As we have seen, the notion of human rights has long been present in Islamic law and was historically upheld by the Muslim states. However, the emergence of human rights as a distinct discourse and independent discipline is a relatively recent phenomenon in Islamic civilization. Three key factors have contributed to this development: (1) the rise of the modern nation-state, which centralized authority and required new legal frameworks, (2) efforts to codify and canonize the Islamic law to address evolving administrative needs, and (3) the global influence of Western human rights discourse, which prompted Muslim thinkers to engage with these concepts in new ways.

In today's modern state contexts, where many Muslim-majority countries operate under secular constitutions and laws with no Islamic basis in their governance, this historical model has been largely abandoned. The modern state monopolizes authority and law-making, necessitating the protection of individual rights against state power. In such contexts, human rights violations arise not from the religious or secular nature of governance but from structural imbalances in power.

In fact, the newly emerged Islamic states after the collapse of the Ottoman state did not invent new sets of rights; rather, they enacted rights that already existed in Islamic law from the outset. An example of this is the Pakistan constitution, which accepts the five fundamental rights promoted by Islamic law. That being said, efforts to Islamize the law and especially the implementation of Islamic criminal law have been criticized in some ways by human rights defenders.

On the other hand, on the international level, Muslim countries generally signed the declarations prepared by the UN. In addition, they also prepared separate documents. The Universal Declaration of Islamic Human Rights, first prepared by the Islamic Council in 1981, was announced at a UNESCO gathering in Paris.[17] Fundamental rights and freedoms were enumerated under a total of 23 headings. The Islamic Council previously aimed to contribute to the issue of human rights by publishing a sample Islamic constitution.

The Organization of Islamic Cooperation (OIC) started its work on this issue by putting human rights on the agenda in 1979. The members of the preparatory committee introduced the human rights project in Islam in 25 articles in 1980.

This document is widely regarded as the first modern attempt to codify human rights within an Islamic framework. Finalized in 1990, it was endorsed by the foreign ministers attending the nineteenth Islamic Conference and was subsequently published by the Organization of Islamic Cooperation (OIC) under the title *The Cairo Declaration on Human Rights in Islam.*

Human rights movements exist in all Muslim-majority countries, though they are more established in places like Pakistan and Egypt, and relatively newer in North Africa and the Middle East. In many of these nations, not only is legal recognition for these groups lacking, but they also face significant governmental pressure. Some countries even strictly prohibit human rights organizations and deny access to international observers. Governments often promote human rights outwardly to improve their global image, while simultaneously silencing those who attempt to expose the realities of rights violations. These policies fluctuate depending on the political climate.

The negative attitude towards human rights is not limited to the pressure of governments. Similarly, some opposition groups and media see and criticize the concept of human rights as a Western construct. At the same time, however, many politicians and writers, including those who are religiously inclined, have begun to use the discourse of human rights and accept the issue as part of their political and academic agenda.

Primordial Origins of Rights

The idea of human rights is the common legacy of humanity since the beginning of human life on earth. While history has witnessed distortions, injustices, and repeated tampering with divinely revealed principles, the essential idea of human dignity and rights has remained a recurring truth across time. This perspective informs the Islamic approach to the origins of human rights. Muslim jurists have never claimed to be the original authors of universal human rights; rather, they have understood their role as restoration and being the custodians and revivers of an authentic, divinely grounded moral legacy entrusted to humanity since its inception.

In this chapter, we have examined the concept of human rights through a sociological lens, tracing its genealogy and examining how these rights have evolved and been framed across various cultural, religious, and political contexts. It has shown how the Islamic law systematized principles of human dignity, inviolability, liberty, and ownership centuries before similar concepts were articulated in Western traditions. Islamic thought, as briefly introduced here and to be further explored in the subsequent chapters, presents a unique model where human dignity and inviolability are not just legal constructs but are integral components of social life and political systems, grounded in the concept of *ādamiyyah* and supported by a legal tradition that emphasizes the sanctity of life and the rights of all individuals.

This analysis calls for a deeper reflection on how the concept of rights can be more authentically integrated into the structures of ethics, law, governance, and social systems of our time. The perspective outlined here lays the foundation for the chapters that follow, which will explore how Islamic thought offers a complementary framework for addressing the challenges and promises of basic rights in the contemporary world.

Notes

1. For these critiques, see Jeroen Vlug, "The Islamic Pursuit of Human Dignity: Revisiting Fundamental Rights Theories in Islamic Law and Legal Philosophy," *Cross-cultural Human Rights Review* 2, no. 1 (2020): 23-48; Declan O'Sullivan, "The Arab, European, Inter-American and African Perspectives on Understanding Human Rights: The Debate Between Universalism and Cultural relativism," *Mediterranean Journal of Human Rights* 8, no. 1 (2004): 153-194; Declan O'Sullivan, "Is the Declaration of Human Rights Universal?" *The International Journal of Human Rights* 4, no. 1 (2000): 25–53.
2. For a more elaborate discussion on Orientalism in the context of human rights studies, see Jeroen Vlug, "The Islamic Pursuit of Human Dignity: Revisiting Fundamental Rights Theories in Islamic Law and Legal Philosophy," *Cross-cultural Human Rights Review* 2, no. 1 (2020): 23-48.
3. For a survey and analysis of various approaches to human rights, see Arnold Yasin Mol, "Islamic Human Rights Discourse and Hermeneutics of Continuity," *Journal of Islamic Ethics* 3, no. 1-2 (2019): 180-206.
4. John Locke, *Two Treatises of Government,* edited by Peter Laslett (Cambridge: Cambridge University Press, 1960), 311.
5. C. G. Weeramantry, *Islamic Jurisprudence: An International Perspective*. (New York: St. Martin's Press, 1988), 113-14.
6. Weeramantry, 105.
7. Léon Ostrorog, *The Angora Reform: Three Lectures Delivered at the Centenary Celebrations of University College on June 27, 28 & 29, 1927,* (London: H. Milford, Oxford University Press, 1927), 30.
8. Donald M. Borchert, ed. *Encyclopedia of Philosophy*. 2nd ed. Vol. 5. (Detroit: Thomson Gale, 2006), s.v. "John Locke," 374; Weeramantry, 105.
9. Al-Dabūsī, *Taqwīm al-Adillah fī Uṣūl al-Fiqh*, ed. Khalīl Muḥyī al-Dīn al-Mays, (Beirut: Dār al-Kutub al-ʿIlmiyyah, 2001), 417; al-Sarakhsī, *Uṣūl al-Sarakhsī*, ed. Abū al-Wafāʾ al-Afghānī, (Beirut: Dār al-Fikr, 2005), vol. 2, 334.
10. Nehama Leibowitz, "New Studies in VaYikra (Leviticus)," *World Zionist Organization*, 1995, pp. 366-367.
11. Bryan Wilson, *Religion in Sociological Perspective* (Oxford and New York: Oxford University Press, 1982).
12. Wael B. Hallaq, *Sharīʿa: Theory, Practice, Transformations* (New York: Cambridge University Press, 2009).

13. See Samy Ayoub, "The Mecelle, Sharia, and the Ottoman State: Fashioning and Refashioning of Islamic Law in the Nineteenth and Twentieth Centuries," *Journal of the Ottoman and Turkish Studies Association* 2, no. 1 (2015): 121-146.
14. Aḥmad ibn Ḥanbal, *Musnad Ahmad*, Book 5, Ḥadīth 512, vol. 1, Ḥadīth 1095, edited by Shuʿayb al-Arnaʾūṭ, (Beirut: Muʾassasat al-Risālah, 1998).
15. See Majid Khadduri, *War and Peace in the Law of Islam* (Baltimore: The Johns Hopkins Press, 1955), 16-18.
16. The concept of the state of exception, as articulated by Carl Schmitt in *On Dictatorship* (1921) and *Political Theology* (1922), defines sovereignty as the power to suspend the law in times of crisis. This notion has been further explored by Giorgio Agamben in the *State of Exception* (2005), who examines how emergency measures can be extended to justify extralegal actions, state violence, and the erosion of fundamental rights. In contrast, nomocracy allows for no such state of exception—divine law remains binding at all times, preventing rulers from invoking crises to expand their power or override legal and moral constraints.
17. For a translation of this declaration, See Salem Azzam, "Universal Declaration of Islamic Human Rights." *The International Journal of Human Rights* 2, no. 3 (1998): 102-112.

CHAPTER TWO

Human Rights in Islamic Law

Ḥuqūq al-Ādamiyyīn

"Indeed, We have dignified the children of Adam."

The Qur'an, *Sūrah al-Isrā'*, 70

The study of human rights necessitates a careful examination of the concepts and terminologies used across different legal and philosophical traditions. The concept of "human rights" is an abstract idea that is widely acknowledged, yet its expression and definition vary depending on historical, cultural, and legal contexts. A genealogical analysis of terms such as "rights," "natural rights," "human rights," and "universal human rights" reveals distinct definitions shaped by various traditions that reflect their own ethical, legal, and philosophical underpinnings.

Building on this understanding, the chapter will explore how Islamic law, through its distinctive terminologies and ethical framework, contributes to the global discourse on human rights. By analyzing key concepts like *ādamiyyah* (humanity) and *'iṣmah* (inviolability), we will uncover how Islamic legal theory conceptualizes and safeguards human dignity. This theoretical exploration will highlight how Muslim jurists have approached the rights of both Muslims and non-Muslims, laying the foundation for the broader analysis that follows in subsequent chapters.

Before exploring the relationship between the classical concepts of *ʿiṣmah* (inviolability) and *ādamiyyah* (humanity), a brief introduction will be useful for those unfamiliar with these terms. These concepts, unfortunately, have not received the attention they deserve in the academic community. There are almost no studies focusing on the concepts of *ʿiṣmah* and *ādamiyyah* as they are used in Islamic law (*fiqh*) and theology (*kalām*).[1]

Ādamiyyah: The Concept of Universal Humanity

In Arabic, a man is called *ādamī* while a woman is called *ādamiyyah*.[2] *Ādamiyyah*, which is both an infinitive verb and an adjective, signifies both being a human and being a child of Adam.[3] The concept of *ādamiyyah* positions every human being as a child of Adam or a member of the family of Adam. From this perspective, all human beings are essentially siblings.

The term *ādamiyyah* is an abstraction used by Muslim jurists (*fuqahāʾ*) to refer to the notion of "humanity" that includes both men and women, as well as both Muslims and non-Muslims. The concept of *ādamiyyah* as a universal category upon which human rights are based is most often attributed to the Ḥanafī school of legal thought. Supported by the Ḥanbalī and Mālikī schools as well, *ādamiyyah* serves as the foundation for fundamental human rights in Islamic law, such as owning property, establishing a family, and forming contracts.[4]

The term *ʿiṣmah* (inviolability) is better known as a theological concept that denotes the infallibility of the prophets, according to the Sunnīs, and of the Shīʿī imams, according to the Shīʿa.[5] It is mentioned in many places in the

Qur'an. The Prophet Muhammad ﷺ uses this term in prophetic narrations (*ḥadīth*) as well. Muslim jurists agree that a person who is entitled to inviolability enjoys what is called in modern human rights law "basic rights" or "inalienable rights." These rights have a different status in Islamic law compared to other types of rights. Muslim jurists called these kinds of rights *ḍarūriyyāt*, literally meaning "indispensable rights" or "axiomatic rights," to demonstrate that they are the most basic and non-negotiable rights in the sense that an honorable human life is impossible without them.

Classical Islamic jurists agree that the protection of human rights is the aim of all legal systems. Therefore, these rights are also called "the objectives of law" (*maqāṣid al-sharīʿah*). As a result, none of the Muslim jurists of the classical era claimed that Islam was the first religion to grant these rights to people. In fact, they have argued that granting these rights equally to all people has always been a common feature of all religions and legal systems throughout human history, beginning with the Prophet Adam.

Ḥaqq and Ḥuqūq: The Concept of Rights

The concept of rights (*ḥaqq*, pl. *ḥuqūq*) has been present in Islamic law and legal theory since its inception. The term *ḥaqq* translates to "right" in English, yet its meaning encompasses a broader semantic range, including reality, sound narrations, the right way, true knowledge, true faith, true evidence, fact, justice, and duty. Notably, *al-Ḥaqq* is also one of the names of God in Islamic tradition. The term *ḥaqq* appears 247 times in the Qur'an and is frequently mentioned in the sayings of the Prophet Muhammad ﷺ.

Ḥuqūq, the plural of *ḥaqq*, is also the standard term used for "law" and the legal sciences in many contemporary Muslim-majority languages, including Arabic and Turkish. In classical Islamic legal discourse, human rights are typically referred to as *ḥuqūq al-ādamiyyīn* (the rights of human beings) or *ḥuqūq al-nās* (the rights of people). In contemporary Islamic legal systems, the term *ḥuqūq al-insān* (the rights of the human being) has become the normative expression. This reflects both the continuity and the evolution of the concept within modern legal frameworks.

Since the question of how Islam views human rights is primarily a matter of law, it should be examined in the context of Islamic jurisprudence (*fiqh*). There are many Qur'anic verses and prophetic narrations on the subject, but these do not directly or fully reflect how the subject is dealt with and implemented within the Islamic legal system. The verses and prophetic narrations are only two of the sources used, alongside other legal (*sharʿī*) proofs, including consensus (*ijmāʿ*), legal analogy (*qiyās*) and public interest (*istiṣlāḥ*).[6]

The approach of Islamic law to human rights can only be fully understood by looking at both abstract rules and concrete historical practices. It is impossible to understand a law that is isolated from historical practice. Therefore, in order to better understand the approach of Islamic law to human rights, legal and sociological perspectives should be used together instead of a narrow approach based solely on Islamic legal texts.

In order to understand the approach of *fiqh* to human rights, it is necessary to emphasize that Islamic law uses a "multi-layered" and "multi-valued" legal logic. In Islamic law, verdicts (*aḥkām*) are divided into three categories: axiomatic verdicts (*ḍarūriyyāt*), scriptural verdicts (*naṣṣiyyāt*) and reasoned verdicts (*ijtihādiyyāt*). Axiomatic verdicts are defined as the eternal, universal, and indisputable principles of law. Scriptural verdicts are verdicts given by God and His Prophet through the Qur'an and *ḥadīth*. Reasoned verdicts are verdicts established by the legal reasoning (*ijtihād*) of the master jurists (*mujtahidūn*). The categories of scriptural and reasoned verdicts together could be called *ẓanniyyāt* (as opposed to axiomatic verdicts). *Ẓanniyyāt* are verdicts that are uncertain because there may not always be certainty with regard to the interpretation of religious textual sources (*naṣṣ*) and legal reasoning (*ijtihād*).

Another point to consider is that if, according to the historians of religion, Islam is a Western religion that comes from the Abrahamic tradition, and if Islamic philosophy has internalized and transcended Greek philosophy, just like Islamic science is a Western science, then why should Islamic law not be viewed as part of the Western legal tradition? Whether being Western is good or bad is a separate issue, but Islamic law is a universal law as Islam is a universal religion. Many human rights concepts, which are mostly associated with secular Western law, are also expressed in classical Islamic legal thought, albeit using different terminology.

An Islamic Perspective on the Human Being

From the perspective of classical Islamic jurisprudence (*fiqh*), human rights are directly linked to the concept of the human being and the purpose of human existence. According to the Qur'an, all people are born as vicegerents (*khalīfah*) of God on earth, a status that is intrinsic to human nature and cannot be revoked, transferred, or delegated.

In order to fulfill the responsibilities inherent in this role, individuals must have certain rights and freedoms. These rights are not privileges granted by the state or society but are universally endowed by God. As such, they cannot be taken away by any authority or transferred to another individual.

ʿAbd al-ʿAziz al-Bukhari (d. 1330) defines a human being by referring to the purpose of creation of an *ādamī* (i.e., a person or human):

> The purpose (meaning) of the life of human beings, for which they were created, such as worshiping God and acting as His viceregents (*khalīfah*), is to fulfill His rights on earth and to shoulder the responsibility of caring for the God-given trust (*amānah*).[7]

Citizens in Islam, as all human beings, are seen as the vicegerents of God, and they are not responsible for unconditional obedience to the head of the state, who is seen as the vicegerent of the Prophet Muhammad ﷺ. On the contrary, the authority of a head of state has clearly drawn boundaries. When rebellion against the Creator is required, the created must not be obeyed.

In other words, political authority is legitimate only when it is exercised with justice. It is through justice that the head of state earns the right to govern. When justice is absent, that legitimacy dissolves, and the obligation to obey the ruler and state officials no longer holds.

This notion of limiting state authority, which determines the relationship between the state and citizens, only emerged in the West during the modern era. The recognition that human beings possess certain inalienable rights, that political power must be constrained, and that the state has no right to intrude arbitrarily upon individual lives became widespread only with the rise of modern liberal thought and the institutionalization of basic freedoms.

Historically, the discourse on human rights arose as a response to the imbalance of power between the individual and the modern state. In such an asymmetrical relationship, the individual was left vulnerable and unprotected in the face of overwhelming state authority. Human rights emerged to redress this imbalance and to safeguard individual dignity and autonomy.

In Islamic law, the protection of individual dignity and inviolability has long been institutionalized through legal doctrines. Among these is the doctrine of *ʿiṣmah*, which is a foundational principle in Islamic criminal jurisprudence. The principle of *ʿiṣmah* affirms the personal inviolability of every individual. Punishments prescribed under this system are known as *ḥudūd*, which literally means "limits" or "protections." Unlike modern conceptions of criminal punishment, which aim at deterrence or retribution, the *ḥudūd* are divine boundaries meant to safeguard essential human and social values.

The violation of *ʿiṣmah* is one of the key terms in Islamic criminal law. The punishment for violating the right to life (*ʿiṣmah al-dam* or *ʿiṣmah al-nafs*) is either compensation or retaliation. Cutting off the right hand was the punishment for a major and obvious violation of the right to property. Flogging or stoning to death were punishments for rape or adultery in the context of the violation of family rights (*ʿiṣmah al-nasl*) in the society.

The penalty for slandering a woman by accusing her of sexual immorality was eighty lashes, as slander was seen as a violation of the right to honor (*ʿiṣmah al-ʿirḍ*). Openly drinking alcohol in the public sphere would be punished with eighty lashes because it was seen as a violation of the preservation of the mind (*ʿiṣmah al-ʿaql*). However, the penalty for drinking alcohol was not applied to non-Muslims who were permitted to drink according to their own religion.

In Islamic history, only the official courts have imposed these penalties when necessary. Moreover, according to Islamic law, these penalties cannot be enforced in the absence of the Islamic state. The Ottomans seldom applied these penalties. Instead, the Ottoman scholars (*ʿulamāʾ*) chose to apply customary law (*ʿurf*) to decide which punishment should be given for a particular criminal offense. This practice is known *taʿzīr* in classical Islamic law. This approach is consistent with the legislation and spirit of Islamic law and should not be perceived as a departure from it. In our contemporary times, these forms of punishment have been replaced by modern legal penalties in the majority of Muslim countries.

The plaintiff may reduce penalties such as retaliation and compensation in the case of a physical assault or murder. Therefore, such penalties fall under the category of personal rights (*ḥuqūq al-ʿibād*). Conversely, if a criminal is found guilty of rape, theft or slander against a chaste woman, the plaintiff cannot reduce the sentence. This category is literally referred to as "the rights of God" (*ḥuqūq Allah*), meaning public rights. These rights are also called "legal rights" (*ḥuqūq al-sharʿ*).

The existence of these penalties in relation to each protected right and the obligation of an official court to enforce them shows that the rights within the scope of the doctrine of *ʿiṣmah* are not merely moral and religious commands (while they are in most other religions). The existence of the Islamic state and the necessary judicial processes are prerequisites for the enforcement and protection of these rights through sanctions of the official courts and police system. In fact, the legitimacy of political authority in an Islamic society stems from the protection of the inviolability of citizens and humanity in general.

Who is the Subject of Rights?: The Human Being or the Citizen

Muslim scholars have disagreed about the subject of law, or more specifically, about who is the subject that has rights and responsibilities. While all human beings are inherently dignified in Islamic thought, the key distinction lies in the state's role and responsibility in protecting and enforcing these rights. I view this difference not as a strict dichotomy between Muslim jurists but rather as varying degrees of universalism in their legal perspectives.

According to one group of scholars, the subject of law is the universal human being (*ādamī*), regardless of any religious belief and political affiliation. According to another group of scholars, the subject of the law is the citizen. Both approaches represent a distinct legal paradigm that adopts a different view on the legal status of human beings and the basic rights that are ascribed to them.

According to many Islamic legal scholars, particularly the Ḥanafī school, Islamic law recognizes all human beings as the subjects of law, assigning them rights and responsibilities equally, without distinction based on citizenship, religion, or territorial affiliation. This perspective is also supported by some Mālikī and Ḥanbalī jurists, who argue that Muslims are obligated to respect and uphold the rights of all human beings, regardless of where they live or their political affiliation. Fundamental rights are not contingent on territorial jurisdiction or state enforcement; rather, they are universal.

In contrast, the Shāfiʿī school does not dispute that all humans have inherent dignity and rights but emphasizes that the state is responsible only for protecting and enforcing the rights of its citizens or those under its jurisdiction. This distinction is grounded in the legal principle that *inviolability is based on faith or the contract of protection* (*al-ʿiṣmah bi-l-īmān aw amān*). According to this principle, Muslims are citizens by virtue of their faith and enjoy full legal rights and protections. Non-Muslims can obtain legal protection through *amān.* Those outside the jurisdiction of the Islamic state are not entitled to the same legal protections, as the state does not have authority over them.

Here, *amān* refers to a formal agreement of protection, such as citizenship, residency, or a visa, through which non-Muslims, such as Jews or Christians, could obtain legal security and state protection within the Islamic governance system. In the Shāfiʿī legal framework, religious identity and contractual protection (*amān*) are the foundation of citizenship. Only those who possess *īmān* (faith) or have entered into a protection contract (*amān*) with the Islamic state are considered full legal subjects, entitled to the full scope of rights and responsibilities under its jurisdiction. This perspective links legal subjecthood to political membership, meaning that citizenship rather than universal humanity is the primary determinant of legal protections and obligations.

On the other hand, according to the majority approach, upheld by the Ḥanafī, Mālikī, and Ḥanbalī schools, Islamic law is universal in its scope, and its subject pertains to all human beings (*ādamiyyah*), regardless of the jurisdiction under which they live. In this view, being human is the primary criterion for determining rights and responsibilities, rather than citizenship, political boundaries, or religious identity. Since all individuals share the fundamental status of being human, their rights are recognized irrespective of whether they are men or women, Muslims or non-Muslims, citizens or non-citizens.

While these two perspectives differ on the role of the state in enforcing rights, they do not fundamentally disagree on the inherent dignity of all human beings. The Qur'anic worldview clearly establishes that all humans are honored and possess rights. The point of divergence is whether it is the duty of the Islamic state to actively enforce and protect those rights for all people, or only for those within its governance.

Who Possesses Basic Rights?: Human Beings or Citizens?

The distinction between the majority and Shāfiʿī approaches has significant legal and ethical implications, particularly regarding who is entitled to state protection of their rights. Both perspectives acknowledge that all human beings possess basic rights, but they differ on whether it is the duty of the state to enforce and protect those rights universally or only within its jurisdiction.

Despite this difference in enforcement, all Islamic schools of law agree on the six fundamental rights (*ḍarūriyyāt*), which form the foundation of Islamic law:

1. The right to inviolability of life (*ʿiṣmah al-nafs* or *al-dam)*.
2. The right to inviolability of property (*ʿiṣmah al-māl*).
3. The right to inviolability of religion (*ʿiṣmah al-dīn*).
4. The right to inviolability of intellect (*ʿiṣmah al-ʿaql*).
5. The right to inviolability of family (*ʿiṣmah al-nasl*).
6. The right to inviolability of honor (*ʿiṣmah al-irḍ*).

The divergence lies not in whether non-citizens have rights but rather in whether the state is obligated to enforce those rights. In short, the majority, which recognizes *ādamiyyah* as the subject of law, ascribes the right to inviolability, which is referred to as *ʿiṣmah*, to humans in general. The Shāfiʿī school, on the other hand, ascribes the right to inviolability only to the citizens of the nation, those who have *īmān* and *amān,* who are regarded as the subject of the law. This spectrum of universalism reflects different interpretations of the state's responsibility in protecting rights rather than a fundamental disagreement over whether human dignity itself is inherent.

It is possible to say that the majority view was founded on the basis of *ādamiyyah*, while the Shāfiʿī school was founded on the basis of what could be called *ibrāhimiyyah*.[8] This is because the Shāfiʿī jurists allocated rights merely to the so-called "People of the Book" (*ahl al-kitāb*), adherents to those monotheistic religions that Islam considers as having received a divine revelation, such as Christianity and Judaism. Those religious adherents who do not belong to the category of the People of the Book, in the Shāfiʿī approach, should not be granted protection and citizenship. The Shāfiʿī or communalist approach, in fact, adopts a universalist approach based on *Ibrāhimiyyah*.

According to the Islamic jurists who adopt the universalist approach based on *ādamiyyah*, the *de facto* relationship between Muslims and non-Muslims is based on peace. That is, unless Muslims are attacked by a non-Muslim hostile army, Muslims cannot attack them. However, according to Muslim jurists who adopt the territorial approach, the natural relationship between Muslims and non-Muslims is one of a state of neutrality or war unless a peace agreement is established in the form of a *dhimmī* contract.[9]

In terms of women's rights, there is no difference between all schools of Islamic law with regard to the basic axiomatic rights (*ḍarūriyyāt*) of women. Sex difference has no place whatsoever in the approach of all schools towards the holders of rights at the level of basic rights. Neither *ādamiyyah* nor *īmān* and *amān* are characteristics related to sex. All people, regardless of whether they are men (*ādamī*) or women (*ādamīyyah*), are accepted as an *ādamī*, a human being.

Are Basic Rights Granted or Acquired?

Another key consequence of the universalist approach grounded on *ādamiyyah* and *ibrāhimiyyah* is whether rights are inherent by birth or granted through legal recognition. According to the *ādamiyyah* approach, inviolability (*ʿiṣmah*) is an inherent right that all human beings possess by birth. Rights are not conferred by the state but are granted directly by God. Here, the relationship between God and humans is the foundation of legal rights rather than the relationship between the state and its citizens. Since these rights originate outside the realm of political authority, no state or ruler has the power to revoke them. In this model, human rights are inalienable: they exist independently of political recognition and cannot be taken away by any authority, whether a government, a ruler, or a legal institution. This perspective places moral and legal constraints on state power.

In contrast, the *ibrāhimiyyah* approach acknowledges that all human beings possess dignity by birth, but it holds that the recognition and enforcement of their rights by the state are contractual. While dignity (*karāmah*) is inherent, legal protections are not automatically granted to everyone; rather, they are acquired through a formal relationship with the state. According to this perspective, the state is the guarantor of legal protections, and rights exist within the framework of citizenship and governance. Individuals receive legal protection if they meet certain conditions, namely being a Muslim (*īmān*) and having a protected status as a non-Muslim (*amān*).

The *ādamiyyah* and *ibrāhimiyyah* approaches differ in how they interpret the legal nature of the *dhimmah* contract, whether it serves as a confirmation of pre-existing rights or as a state-granted privilege. From the *ādamiyyah* viewpoint, every human being possesses inherent rights and duties by virtue of their humanity (*ādamiyyah*), what might be termed today as "personal rights." Under this framework, the *dhimmah* contract does not create new rights for non-Muslims but rather formalizes pre-existing ones. It is a written confirmation of their natural right to inviolability (*ʿiṣmah*) rather than a conditional concession granted by the state.

From this perspective, the *jizyah* (non-Muslim tax) is not a form of subjugation but a tax obligation parallel to those imposed on Muslims.[10] Just as Muslims are obligated to pay *zakāt* and other state taxes, non-Muslims fulfill their financial duty to the state through *jizyah*. The distinction lies not in the inequality of rights but in the differentiation of tax obligations based on religious and legal categories.

In contrast, the *ibrāhimiyyah* approach does not recognize rights as inborn or independent of the state. Instead, it sees the *dhimmah* contract as a formal agreement through which the state grants inviolability (*ʿiṣmah*) to non-Muslims. In this model, legal protections, including life, property, and religious freedom, are not inherent human rights but contractual privileges conferred by the state upon its citizens. Under this framework, the *dhimmah* contract is not merely a confirmation of an existing right but rather an act of political recognition. The state acknowledges non-Muslims as citizens only upon entering into this contract, thereby granting them protection in exchange for their legal and financial obligations, including the payment of *jizyah*.

Classifying Rights

In contemporary global discourse, rights are generally classified into three categories: *human rights* that apply to all human beings by virtue of their humanity; *legal rights* which are granted to individuals as citizens or residents of a particular state; and *moral rights* which represent ethical claims but are not necessarily enforceable by law.

Some scholars further classify human rights into *legal* and *moral* human rights. In this view, human rights may be understood as universal moral or ethical claims.[11] When these rights are codified in legislation or recognized by institutions, they are transformed into legal rights that are enforceable either through domestic or international legal mechanisms. As such, human rights have been formally adopted through international treaties, regional charters, national constitutions, conventions, and declarations.[12]

In this sense, legal rights are moral rights that have been institutionalized within a legal system.[13] Nevertheless, human rights are always understood to be universal as they belong equally to all human beings by virtue of their humanity. States enforce these rights as legal obligations, while moral rights that remain uncodified may still carry significant weight through religious, cultural, or social norms and sanctions.

In Islamic law, rights are traditionally categorized into three main types, each grounded in distinct legal and ethical foundations. These are: *ḍarūrī* (essential) rights, *tashrīʿī* (legislated) rights, and *akhlāqī* (ethical) rights. *Ḍarūrī* rights refer to essential, universal entitlements granted to all human beings. They include what Muslim legal scholars have identified as the five or, in some views, six fundamental rights:

protection of religion (*dīn*), life (*nafs*), intellect (*ʿaql*), lineage (*nasl*), property (*māl*), and honor (*ʿirḍ*). These rights are foundational to the *Sharīʿah* and are considered absolute and non-negotiable. Their preservation is a primary objective of the law and a duty upon both individuals and the state. *Tashrīʿī* rights are those legislated by the state for specific purposes or groups, based on legal precedent, administrative necessity, or public interest (*maṣlaḥah*). These rights include, for instance, entitlements related to taxation, public office, or service benefits. Unlike *ḍarūrī* rights, *tashrīʿī* rights are subject to change according to context and circumstance, and may differ across societies and periods. *Akhlāqī* rights include the rights of parents, spouses, neighbors, guests, and other forms of interpersonal obligation that are not enforced by the judiciary but are binding in the court of conscience and religion. While they may not be codified or enforced by the state, they are considered no less important within the Islamic moral universe. From a legal-theoretical standpoint, these categories reflect varying degrees of normative weight. *Ḍarūrī* rights are considered axiomatic and universal, which form the foundational principles of Islamic law. *Tashrīʿī* and *akhlāqī* rights are derived from Qur'anic verses and prophetic narrations, as well as legal reasoning (*ijtihād*) by scholars.

Islamic law also distinguishes between inherent and acquired rights at the individual level. Inherent rights are inborn and permanent; they arise from a person's status as a human being. These fall under the doctrine of *ʿiṣmah* because these rights are thought to be inborn in each individual. Such rights cannot be revoked, suspended, or forfeited, because they are tied to the essence of human existence.

Acquired rights arise through contracts, agreements, or legally recognized transactions between individuals. Because they are conditional upon such arrangements, they may be forfeited if the terms are violated or nullified. In contrast, inherent rights are intrinsic to the human condition; they cannot be lost, suspended, or revoked, for a person cannot be stripped of their humanity. These rights are not confined to a specific verse of the Qur'ān or a particular prophetic narration but are drawn from the overarching spirit of the *Sharī'ah*. Through a comprehensive engagement with the religious sources (*naṣṣ*) and sound legal reasoning (*ijtihād*), Muslim jurists have affirmed these rights as fundamental to human dignity.

Applications in History

The different approaches to human rights discussed so far have been applied under various Islamic political administrations across different regions and historical periods. Among the most prominent examples are the Umayyads, Abbasids, the Umayyads of Andalusia, the Mughals of the Indian Subcontinent, and the Ottomans. Each of these civilizations implemented Islamic legal principles in ways that reflected their socio-political realities while engaging with the broader discourse of justice, rights, and governance.

In the nineteenth century, the Ottomans observed the shifting legal and political conditions of the time and instigated reforms based on a reformist (*iṣlāḥ*) or revivalist (*tajdīd*) approach. These reforms were regarded by the Ottoman statesmen and religious scholars (*'ulamā'*) as an expression of the universal rights approach in *fiqh*, albeit expressed in a new terminology.

The Caliph, *shaykh al-Islām*, and the majority of religious scholars did not perceive the reforms in question as a departure from Islam.[14] Rather, they saw them as an articulation of existing Islamic principles in a modern legal language. For this reason, instead of opposing these reforms, most scholars endorsed them and recognized their continuity with the classical Islamic legal tradition.[15]

Historically, Muslims built multi-religious and multi-civilizational political systems upon the universalist approach to Islamic law. This approach, which was successfully applied for centuries across diverse regions, derived its legal and philosophical foundation from the principle of inviolability by virtue of humanity (*al-ʿiṣmah bi-l-ādamiyyah*).

However, this legacy is at risk of being forgotten. In order for Muslims to contribute to contemporary rights discourse, it is essential that the universalist legal framework, which is based on the principles of *ādamiyyah* (humanity) and *ʿiṣmah* (inviolability), regains its centrality within contemporary Islamic thought. This would allow Islamic legal tradition to once again offer a unique and ethically grounded vision of justice, rights, and human dignity in the contemporary world.

Does Islamic Law Protect Those Who Deny Islam?

The aforementioned Islamic universalist perspective on human rights applies to all individuals, irrespective of their adherence to Islam. This inclusivity extends even to those who deny the final religion of God, Islam, His final messenger, Muhammad ﷺ, and His Book, the Qur’an. This perspective raises profound questions: Why did God and the Prophet Muhammad ﷺ grant freedom and human rights to those who denied them? Why does Islamic law protect those who deny Islam?

The answer lies in the Islamic understanding of the divine purpose behind the creation of the universe, its inhabitants, and the existence of paradise and hellfire. God's creative act is intended to test human beings through their conduct on earth, with the promise of eventual reward or punishment. However, accountability for one's actions during this test can only be meaningful if individuals are granted complete freedom and the right to inviolability. Only free agents can truly deserve a reward for choosing righteous actions over wrong ones, and similarly, only those who act freely can justly be punished for wrong choices when the right path is available. Without this complete freedom, the very concepts of paradise and hellfire would lose their significance for human beings.

The primary objective of Islamic governance and legal frameworks is to establish a just social-political order where individuals have the freedom to exercise their free will, a prerequisite for moral accountability before God in the Hereafter. To facilitate this, Islamic law safeguards six essential human rights: the inviolability of life, property, religion, intellect, family, and honor. However, Islamic law does not employ coercion to dictate faith or an individual's relationship with God. The Qur'an and the *ḥadīth* of Prophet Muḥammad ﷺ criticize false beliefs and unjust practices, but do so through reasoned argumentation and persuasion, not compulsion. Islam invites individuals to embrace the truth voluntarily, as faith loses its meaning if imposed by force.

The deeper rationale behind this approach is regarding the purpose of creation. The universe and its inhabitants exist as part of a divine test that determines the fate of human beings in paradise or hellfire. However, for this test to be just and fair, human beings must be granted complete freedom and inviolability. Only free moral agents can earn rewards for choosing righteousness over wrongdoing, just as only those who act with genuine free will can be held accountable for rejecting the truth. Without this complete freedom, divine accountability would become meaningless, as people could not be justly rewarded or punished if they were compelled in their beliefs and actions.

Women's Rights in the Context of Ādamiyyah

From the perspective of *ādamiyyah,* men and women share equal status as human beings and enjoy the same fundamental rights derived from their humanity. In the Qur'an and prophetic narrations, no distinction exists between men and women regarding their religious status, moral responsibility, or the consequences of their deeds in the Hereafter. Nor is there a distinction with regard to the religious rewards (*thawāb*) they will obtain from the deeds they perform, the account they will give in the hereafter, and the recompense they will receive. Both women and men are the most honorable of Allah's creatures and have the honor of being the vicegerents of Allah on earth. Both possess intellect, legal personality (*dhimmah*), free will, and dignity.

Thus, men and women are equal in possessing the qualities of *ādamiyyah* and are also equal in their entitlement to all rights entailed by *ādamiyyah.* Aside from these basic rights, there may be certain differences in other areas. In terms of roles and characteristics, Allah Most High has bestowed superiority on women in certain areas and on men in others.

Islamic law has produced a complex system with regard to terminating marriages, dissimilar to the methods and concepts utilized in modern law. Accordingly, marriage contracts can be freely concluded or canceled with the consent of the parties without the supervision of state officials or religious authorities. Ḥanafī law provides equal rights for unilateral divorce (*ṭalāq*). Without a court order, both parties have the authority to reach an agreement in three instances of divorce.

However, according to the Shāfiʿī school, a woman does not have the authority to unilaterally divorce. That being said, both legal schools acknowledged that women have the authority to apply to the court for divorce and in such a case, the divorce would take place according to the court's decision.[16]

The universalist approach based on *ādamiyyah* does not see any fundamental legal difference between women and men. Both are human (*ādamī*) and have the same human rights. However, a person who approaches the subject from a modern perspective sees that women are treated differently from men in areas other than basic human rights, such as inheritance and family law. However, these have not traditionally been viewed as unequal practices. It must not be forgotten that the concept of equality and social gender roles have undergone tremendous changes during the process of modernization. These changes came to be due to the prevalent customs that influence law. Islamic legal thought acknowledges that customs may change over time. Accordingly, some of the legal verdicts, if they are based on customs, can also not remain fixed and may change.

According to Ḥanafī legal scholars, a widow or unmarried woman can freely marry on her own, and the marriage contract is not valid without her consent. The Shāfiʿī approach, on the other hand, ascribes genuine authority regarding the marriage of women to their families. According to this approach, the marriage contract is invalid as long as there is no consent of the guardians from the woman's family. A girl cannot marry on her own without her parents' consent, and only a widow is allowed to marry without the consent of her family. The Shāfiʿī approach argued that this measure would protect the interest of women claiming that parents were more experienced than young women in terms of the difficulties of marriage.

It is necessary to correctly understand the Qur'anic verse, which mentions the hitting of an unruly woman as a symbolic preventative measure before a divorce.[17] In order to properly understand this verse, we have to look at how the Prophet Muhammad ﷺ understood and practiced it. Prophet Muhammad ﷺ had never hit a woman. He is the one to whom the Qur'an was revealed. He best understood and practiced it. As a matter of fact, as narrated by the Prophet's ﷺ wife ʿĀʾisha, he never slapped a woman, child, or slave during his life.[18] In addition, there are also many *aḥadīth* that prohibit hitting and beating women. Therefore, beating women is against the Sunna of the Prophet ﷺ and is a sin. The hitting mentioned in the verse is interpreted by scholars as deserting or hitting with a handkerchief or *miswāk*[19] and the like, without causing harm and pain, with the aim of symbolically making clear that the next step will be divorce (*ṭalāq*).

Women, as *ādamiyyah*, fully possess all fundamental rights to inviolability (*ʿiṣmah*) without distinction from men. While differences in legal applications exist, they are tied to social, customary, and legal considerations rather than a denial of women's intrinsic rights or dignity. The best way to understand women's rights in Islam is to start by unearthing the meaning and practical implications of *ḥuqūq al-ādamiyyīn* equally for both men and women.

Notes

1. Baber Johansen noted years ago in an article on the concept of *ʿiṣmah* that it had not yet been the subject of an independent study in the form of a dedicated article or book. For an analysis of *ʿiṣmah* within the Ḥanafī legal tradition, see "Der 'isma-Begriff im hanafitischen Recht" in Johansen, Baber, *Contingency in a Sacred Law: Legal and Ethical Norms in the Muslim Fiqh*, (Leiden: Brill, 1999), 238-262.
2. Note that the feminine form is transliterated in the same manner as the general concept of "humanity" (i.e., *ādamiyyah*). These should not be confused.
3. In the Islamic tradition, Prophet Adam, peace be upon him, is seen as the first human being created by God. Hence, in that sense, all human beings are "children of Adam."
4. See Tareq Sharawi, "How Does Islam Treat People Outside the Abrahamic Religions? Between Ādamiyyah and Ibrāhimiyyah," PhD diss. (Ibn Haldun University, 2020), and of the same author, "The Inviolability of the Non-Muslims in Islamic Law: A Comparative Reading of Modern and Classical Debates," *Afkār: Journal of 'Aqidah and Islamic Thought* 1 (2020): 79-112.
5. The Sunnī and Shiʿa are the two main denominations of Islam. Sunnīs believe inviolability, which in Islamic theology refers to freedom from sin, is a characteristic only the prophets have. This includes all prophets that came before Islam, such as Abraham, Moses and Jesus, peace be upon them all. The Shiʿa, however, also attributed this characteristic to all of the imams they follow stemming from the lineage of ʿAli, the cousin and son-in-law of Prophet Muḥammad, peace be upon him.
6. The Arabic technical term for legal analogy here, *qiyās*, should not be confused with the Aristotelian syllogism as it is used in Arabic logic (*manṭiq*), for which the Muslim logicians (*manṭiqiyyūn*) also used the term *qiyās*. For more on Islamic legal language, see Wael B. Hallaq, *Islamic Legal Theories: An Introduction to Sunnī Uṣūl al-Fiqh* (Cambridge: Cambridge University Press, 1997).
7. "*Wa maʿnā al-ādami huwa mā khuliqa lahu min ʿibādat rabbihi wa al-khilāfati fī arḍihi li-iqāmat ḥuqūqihi wa taḥammul amānātihi*" ʿAbd al-ʿAzīz al-Bukhārī (d. 730 AH), *Kashf al-Asrār ʿan Usūl Fakhr al-Islām al-Bazdawī* (ed. Muḥammad al-Muʿtaṣim billāh al-Baghdādī), Beirut: Dār al-Kitāb al-ʿArabī, 1418/1997, vol. I, 378.

8. Ibrāhīm is the Arabic name for Prophet Abraham, peace be upon him and is considered the spiritual forefather of the three monotheistic religions: Islam, Christianity, and Judaism. Hence, some scholars speak of the "Abrahamic" tradition. For more on this, see Guy G. Stroumsa, *The Making of Abrahamic Religions in Late Antiquity* (New York: Oxford University Press, 2015).

9. *Dhimmī* is a term for the legal status of non-Muslims who are under the protection of the Islamic state and hence pay a special tax, called the *jizyah*, for the protection of their rights.

10. The *jizyah* is a tax paid by non-Muslims in Islamic lands in exchange for their protected status. This was obligatory upon sane adult males, and not upon others, such as women, children, elderly people, religious clergy or those who were handicapped. Also, non-Muslims who only temporarily traveled in the Muslim lands (*musta'min*) for the purposes of trade, for instance, did not have to pay the *jizyah* tax. See, for example, Benjamin Braude, *Christian and Jews in the Ottoman Empire* (Boulder, Colorado and London: Lynne Rienner Publishers, 2014), 4-5.

11. Marie-Bénédicte Dembour, "What Are Human Rights? Four Schools of Thought," *Human Rights Quarterly* 32, No. 1 (2010): 1-20.

12. Hurst Hannum, "The Status of the Universal Declaration of Human Rights in National and International Law," *Georgia Journal of International and Comparative Law* 25, No. 1-2 (1995): 289.

13. Duncan Ivison, Rights (Stocksfield: Acuman, 2008), 30. For a more elaborate discussion on legal and moral rights, see Jeroen Vlug, "The Contested Grounds of Human Rights in Islam and The West: A Comparative Study" (PhD diss., Ibn Haldun University, 2022), 67-77.

14. *Shaykh al-Islam* was the title given to the highest-ranking religious scholar in the Ottoman bureaucracy who, aside from religious authority, had extensive political power as well.

15. See Recep Şentürk and Muhammed Said Bilal, *Human Rights in the Ottoman Reform: Foundations, Motivations and Formations* (İbn Haldun Üniversitesi Yayınları, 2020).

16. For an overview of various perspectives on marriage in classical Islamic law, see Kecia Ali, "Marriage in Classical Islamic Jurisprudence: A Survey of Doctrines," in *The Islamic Marriage Contract: Case Studies in Islamic Family Law*, ed. Asifa Qurayshi and Frank E. Vogel (Cambridge, MA and London, England: Harvard University Press, 2009), 11-45.

17. "*Husbands should take good care of their wives, with [the bounties] God has given to some more than others and with what they spend out of their own money. Righteous wives are devout and guard what God would have them guard in their husbands' absence. If you fear high-handedness from your wives, remind them [of the teachings of God], then ignore them when you go to bed, then hit them. If they obey you, you have no right to act against them: God is most high and great.*" (The Qur'an 4:34)
18. Related in the *ḥadīth*-collection of *Ṣaḥīḥ Muslim*: "*The Messenger of Allah, peace and blessings be upon him, did not strike a servant or a woman, and he never struck anything with his hand.*"
19. A *miswāk* is a natural toothbrush traditionally used in many parts of the Muslim world. The practice of using the *miswāk* for oral hygiene dates back thousands of years and is mentioned in Islamic texts as a recommended way to maintain clean teeth.

العصمة بالآدمية

CHAPTER THREE

I Am Therefore I Have Rights

Al-ʿIṣmah bi al-Ādamiyyah

The relationship between humanity and rights has been a subject of extensive discourse across civilizations, particularly among Islamic and Western legal scholars. At the heart of this discussion lies a fundamental question: Who is entitled to human rights, and on what basis? The answers to this question have varied across legal traditions and historical contexts and shaped diverse conceptions of justice, citizenship, and legal protection. The lack of a universally accepted resolution to this issue continues to fuel political and legal conflicts worldwide, which manifests in debates over the scope and application of human rights.

This theoretical divide between universal rights and civil or citizen rights, as prominent in modern legal discourse, can also be traced back to classical Islamic law from its formative period in the first century of the Islamic calendar onward.[1] A thorough examination of Islamic legal thought, from classical jurists to contemporary scholars, reveals a long-standing discussion on the relationship between inviolability (*ʿiṣmah*) and humanity (*ādamiyyah*). This inquiry uncovers an often-overlooked intellectual tension between the two approaches. The *ādamiyyah* paradigm asserts that inviolability is granted to all human beings solely by virtue of their humanity. The *ibrāhimiyyah* paradigm argues that inviolability is contingent upon faith or contractual allegiance with an Islamic polity.

For an extensive period of time, Islamic law has played an important role in shaping not only the relations within the Islamic community but also the relations between Muslims and non-Muslims in a wider geography. In fact, religious and cultural pluralism was institutionalized by the commands of the Qur'an, which ordered Muslims to be tolerant towards Christians and Jews. Therefore, Islamic civilization became a societal mosaic in which different religious communities managed their own affairs within considerably wide limits.

After the year 1000, great diversity was added to this mosaic through conquests and encounters that brought Islam to the Indian Subcontinent, Southeast Asia, and most of the Central Asian Steppes, as well as Southeast Europe and Sub-Saharan Africa. Many of these lands had a greater degree of religious diversity than the Arabian Peninsula when Islam was revealed. Hence, Islamic law allocated rights to followers of the non-Abrahamic religions as well, such as Hindus, Buddhists, Zoroastrians, and Pagans.[2]

When we analyze the original terminology of classical Islamic law, it becomes clear that the relationship between inviolability (*ʿiṣmah*) and humanity (*ādamiyyah*) plays a key role in understanding the different perspectives among Muslim jurists regarding the state's role in enforcing rights. While classical jurists agreed on which rights fall under *ʿiṣmah* and should be protected, they differed on whether the state has a duty to enforce these rights universally or only within its jurisdiction. This distinction shaped divergent legal approaches to the scope of state responsibility in upholding human rights.

However, several key questions divided them: Who has the right to *ʿiṣmah* and why? Does it belong to humanity as a whole or merely to the Muslims and those who make a peace agreement with them? Does Islamic jurisprudence allow for the making of laws for non-citizens and thus grant them human rights? Is it possible to apply such laws outside of the authority of Islam and beyond the so-called "Abode of Islam" (*dār al-islām*)?[3] Who is included in the legislative sphere of Islamic law, all of humanity or solely the citizens of the Islamic state composed of Muslims and non-Muslims? To what extent and on what basis are Muslims given the right to interact with or obstruct other legal traditions under their rule? The answers to these questions hinge on how jurists conceptualized the relationship between humanity and human rights, particularly regarding the state's role in enforcing those rights and the jurisdictional limits of Islamic law.

As discussed earlier, this legal disagreement carries significant implications. If human rights are understood as belonging to all of humanity, then Muslim individuals, communities, and states bear the responsibility of upholding and defending these rights universally, regardless of jurisdiction or political affiliation. In contrast, if human rights are seen as exclusive to citizens, then the state's obligation is limited to protecting only those under its governance, without a broader duty toward non-citizens. This distinction shapes not only the legal scope of protection but also the ethical and political responsibilities of Muslims in engaging with global justice and human rights discourse.

The Ādamiyyah Paradigm

"Basic rights are due by virtue of being human."

As we mentioned earlier, Abū Ḥanīfa (d. 150/767), Imam Mālik (d. 173/795), Aḥmad ibn Ḥanbal (d. 233/855) and their followers developed a particular theory of universal rights grounded upon the Islamic worldview and values. They are "inalienable," meaning that they cannot be taken away by any authority, a state or otherwise. These rights are given by birth by virtue of being human. They are granted universally and unconditionally to everyone on a permanent and equal basis.

Abū Ḥanīfa attached the concept of humanity (*ādamiyyah*) to the concept of inviolability (*ʿiṣmah*). He argued that descent from the lineage of Prophet Adam, peace be upon him, is the legal basis for fundamental rights *(al-ʿiṣmah bi al-ādamiyyah*), whether one is Muslim or not.[4] Although these concepts require a more detailed explanation, we can express this principle as "*the inviolability of fundamental human rights is the right of all human beings by virtue of their humanity*."

Abū Ḥanīfa's students recorded his views on legal issues, as he did not write any legal works himself. He was more concerned with training legal scholars and thus imbued his students with his legal principles and vision. Abū Ḥanīfa's two leading students, Abū Yūsuf (d. 182/798) and Muḥammad al-Shaybānī (d. 189/805), as well as other students, distilled his legal method from his teachings and conveyed his views to the next generations.

One of the most profound affirmations of universal human dignity and inviolability in the Ḥanafī tradition is found in the works of Abū Zayd al-Dabūsī (d. 430/1039), one of the leading early authorities in Ḥanafī *uṣūl al-fiqh*. Al-Dabūsī explains that when God the Almighty created humanity to bear His trust (*amānah*), He honored them by endowing them with intellect (*ʿaql*) and legal capacity (*dhimmah*), thus making every human being inherently qualified to hold rights and bear responsibilities.[5] According to al-Dabūsī, human dignity, inviolability, freedom, and ownership are fundamental rights of all human beings, granted to them by God as part of their role in carrying divine trust. These rights are not conditioned on religion or social status.

Building on this same foundational principle, Abū Bakr al-Sarakhsī (d. 490/1090), one of the greatest jurists of the Ḥanafī school, elaborates that these rights are inseparable from human existence and begin from birth, regardless of whether a person has yet attained discernment (*tamyīz*) or not. In his al-*Mabsūṭ*, al-Sarakhsī writes:

> "When God created human beings to bear His divine trust, He honored them with intellect and legal capacity, making them eligible for the obligations God placed upon them. He then established for them inviolability, freedom, and ownership, so that they may continue their lives in a manner that enables them to fulfill the responsibility they carry. These rights, inviolability, freedom, and ownership, are inherent in an individual from the moment of birth, and both the discerning and non-discerning are equal in this regard. Thus, the capacity to bear rights and responsibilities is inherent in individuals from birth, and all individuals, regardless of their level of intellectual development, are equal in this respect."[6]

Here, al-Sarakhsī affirms that every human being, by virtue of being human, possesses inherent dignity and rights from birth, before any societal or legal recognition. Whether a person is a child, an adult, or someone with limited mental capacity, they have the basic rights to life, dignity, freedom, and property. These inherent rights form the necessary basis for fulfilling the divine trust for which humanity was created.

Taken together, the positions of al-Dabūsī and al-Sarakhsī present a coherent and robust theory of universal human dignity and rights within the Islamic legal tradition. They establish that human inviolability, freedom, and property are God-given rights that precede and ground all religious and social obligations. These foundational rights do not derive from social contracts, as imagined by Enlightenment thinkers, nor are they conditional upon a person's faith or status in society. Instead, they are grounded in humanity itself (*ādamiyyah*).

This principle of inherent human dignity and inviolability is also clearly affirmed by Ibn Māzah (d. 1141), an early authoritative Ḥanafī jurist, who writes:

الآدميُّ محترمٌ حيّاً وميتاً

"*A human being is to be respected, both in life and in death.*"[7]

Thus, human dignity is not situational but permanent and inseparable from human existence itself, extending beyond life to the honor due to the human body in death. Later, Fakhr al-Dīn al-Zaylaʿī (d. 743/1343) explicitly reinforces this foundational principle by grounding inviolability (*ʿiṣmah*) in humanity (*ādamiyyah*) rather than religious affiliation. He writes:

ولا نسلِّم أنَّ أصلَ العصمة بالإسلام بل بكونه آدمياً

"We do not acknowledge that the basis of inviolability is Islam; rather, it is due to being human (ādamī)."[8]

This profound assertion rejects any claim that inviolability is reserved for Muslims alone and instead affirms that the very essence of being human is the ground for dignity and protection under the law. This view is later echoed by Muḥammad Amīn ibn ʿĀbidīn (d. 1252/1836), one of the most eminent jurists of the later Ḥanafī tradition, who makes the point even more explicit:

الآدمي مُكرَّمٌ شرعاً ولو كافراً

"A human being is dignified in the eyes of the Sharīʿah, even if he is a non-Muslim."[9]

Here, Ibn ʿĀbidīn affirms that dignity (*karāmah*) is an inherent feature of humanity, not something that hinges on religious identity or communal membership, and thereby rejects any religiously-based exclusion from dignity and inviolability. In other words, human inviolability is not granted externally but flows naturally from the very fact of being human, with freedom and dignity being intrinsic to human nature.

These juristic positions, spanning centuries, form a consistent framework that grounds human dignity and inviolability in humanity itself (*ādamiyyah*). Far from being a marginal view, this universalist paradigm shaped major strands of Islamic jurisprudence and governance for centuries. Yet, as Muslim societies moved into the modern era, these classical foundations would need to be rearticulated and adapted to new legal and political realities.

Modern Expressions in Islamic Law

The works of the Ottoman legal scholars of the late period, particularly Ahmed Cevdet Pasha (d. 1312/1895), mark the initial efforts toward the modern regulation and legislation of Ottoman public law. The famous late Ottoman work on Islamic commercial law, *Majallat al-aḥkām al-ʿadliyya* (called *Mecelle* in Ottoman Turkish), shows the same universalist Ḥanafī approach. The *Majalla*'s formation increased the hopes of reformists who saw it as a revival of Islamic law. Unfortunately, with the fall of the Ottoman Empire, this reform movement was put to a halt. Most Muslim jurists, even those committed to the Ḥanafī tradition, have since then ignored the universalist view. As a result, the communalist view became dominant during the twentieth century.

To defend their teachings, universalist Muslim jurists used proofs based on reason and revelation. These proofs are found dispersed in classical Islamic texts, such as works on theology (*kalām*), Islamic law (*fiqh*), and Islamic legal theory (*uṣūl al-fiqh*). The most commonly used evidence to defend the universality of human rights is the universality of Allah's address in the Qur'an and the universality of the Prophet's ﷺ call.

Since Allah's address in the Qur'an is universal and all human beings are thus allowed to respond freely to His invitation, human rights should be universal, too. Furthermore, Allah's aim in creating human beings is to test them. This goal is not realized, and people cannot be held responsible for their behavior unless they are given the right to inviolability and freedom.

The arguments Islamic scholars put forth to defend the universality of rights are based on the idea of the universal human being and his place in the network of social relations. The main aim is to establish peaceful relations, not only between Muslims and non-Muslims but also among non-Muslims from different religions themselves. Many non-Muslim communities of different religions lived under the rule of Muslims in Andalusia, the Ottoman Empire and the Indian Subcontinent. Islamic law was applied to regulate relations not only between Muslims and non-Muslims but also between various non-Muslim communities.

In addition to the rational proofs mentioned above, Ḥanafī jurists also used proofs based on the Qur'an and prophetic narrations (*ḥadīth*) to defend universal human rights. The sacred texts of Islam express universal Divine protection for all of Allah's creatures, for He is the Lord of the Worlds. The Qur'an commands: "*There can be no hostility, except towards aggressors.*"[10] Islam forbids compulsion in religion.[11]

In many verses, Allah commands the protection of His creatures. Humans should be protected because Allah does not want His creatures to perish. This is only possible by granting inviolability to each person.[12] The Qur'an expresses the purpose of creation as: "*Exalted is He who holds all control in His hands; who has power over all things; who created death and life to test you [people] and reveal which of you does best—He is the Mighty, the Forgiving.*" (Qur'an 67: 1-2)

In the Qur'an and the narration of Prophet Muhammad ﷺ, Allah strictly forbade the violation of rights and the murder of people.[13] Qur'anic verses also command the protection of non-Muslim women, children, and religious clergy. We can summarize the rational and scriptural proofs we have listed so far as follows:

- The Divine purpose of creating humanity is to test (*ibtilāʾ*) people and to hold them responsible for their behavior (*taklīf*). However, if people are not given freedom and inviolability, the Divine purpose cannot be realized.
- Allah does not want to harm or destroy His creatures. Therefore, human beings must be protected. This is only possible by giving each of them inviolability.
- In the Qur'an and *ḥadīth,* it is strictly forbidden to attack and murder human beings. In addition, during the war, the protection of non-Muslim women, children, and religious clergy was commanded.
- Unless disbelievers fight against Muslims, disbelief (*kufr*), as such, under normal circumstances, is not a threat to Muslims. Therefore, it should be tolerated.
- Religiously sanctioned war (*jihād*) is not an offensive but a defensive war. Therefore, in the context of peaceful relations, non-Muslims also enjoy inviolability as long as they do not attack Muslims.
- The aim of war is not to destroy the enemy but to establish peace in order to live in security and to be able to freely preach and practice Islam.
- The only reason for a legitimate war is for self-defense in order to protect one's inviolability and sanctity. The mere unbelief of enemies is not a valid reason for war. Therefore, in a state of peace, everyone benefits from inviolability.

- As clearly expressed by the Qur'an, compulsion in religion is forbidden.

The result of this approach is that Muslims have allowed non-Muslim groups under their rule to freely implement their laws, as long as they did not harm any of the protected fundamental human rights. For example, when Egypt was conquered ʿAmr b. al-ʿĀs (d. 43/664)[14] left the indigenous people at liberty to practice their traditional laws. However, he abolished the custom of sacrificing girls to the Nile in order to receive more water because it harmed the inviolability of human life.

Similarly, Hindus in the Indian Subcontinent have had the authority to enforce their own laws, with the exception of the custom of burning a widowed woman with the body of her deceased husband. Muslim rulers abolished these two traditional customs in Egypt and the Indian Subcontinent because they contradicted the right to life.[15] Similarly, the practice of siblings marrying each other, which was part of the traditions of the Zoroastrians of Iran, was abolished because it contradicted the principle of protecting the family.

Scholars who advocated the *Ādamiyyah* paradigm argued that the purpose of God in creating the human family in the world was to provide responsibility (*taklīf*) and that this could not be achieved without being free and protected. Because if people do not have basic freedoms and protection, then their purpose in the world cannot be realized.

A person's religious preference should be respected even if it contradicts the Islamic doctrine. His or her life must be protected, for this is the only way he or she can respond to the Divine call. A person's ideas should similarly be respected, for the intellect is the mechanism that makes ethical choices, whether they are right or wrong. In addition, the intellect is the only means for people to understand and practice the divine message. Therefore, every person's thoughts should be respected and protected, even if they contradict the Muslim creed. This is the reasoning that was utilized by the masters of Islamic law in the classical period to ground and justify the six fundamental rights.

In the case that someone does harm to the inviolability of another person, his or her own inviolability is suspended, albeit not completely or permanently (as *ʿiṣmah* is not taken away indefinitely). Not individuals, but an official court determines the necessary penalty, based on objective laws and principles. However, if public authorities fail to protect the citizen's inviolability, then the individual himself or herself is authorized and responsible for enabling the protection of inviolability. Those who die while fighting to protect his or her inviolability are considered martyrs. In other words, fighting for the sake of human rights, such as life, religion, intellect, family, and property, which are all necessary conditions for a free and fair society, is considered equivalent to the struggle to protect the Islamic lands against their enemies.

The reason for this is that the principle of inviolability is indivisible and cannot be suspended or postponed, regardless of the circumstances, for all people, who, in principle, are considered to have the same fundamental rights equally and continuously.

Only in the case of criminals who are deserving of penal sanction, according to the Ḥanafī scholars, *ʿiṣmah* can be divided. That is, in the criminal process, only a part of the inviolability is suspended for a certain period of time. In other words, only the aspect of inviolability determined by law, specifically related to the penalty, is suspended during the imposition of that penalty, while the rest remains intact. For example, even if a thief is punished for theft, his or her life and property remain inviolable.

The Ḥanafī school was particularly influential in the Indian Subcontinent, Central Asia, Anatolia, and the Balkans during the time of the Ottoman Empire. The legal discourse of the Islamic scholars in the Ottoman period promoted the Ḥanafī approach. Thus, for a long period of time and in a very wide geography, precedence was given to Ḥanafī *fiqh* when governing a multi-religious and multicultural state based on the *millet* system.[16]

Abū Ḥanīfa's influence lasted until the beginning of the twentieth century. For example, the Syrian Ḥanafī scholar ʿAbd al-Ghani al-Maydanī (d. 1298/1881) of Damascus wrote at the end of the nineteenth century that a human being had inviolability merely by virtue of the dignity of his existence (*al-ḥurr maʿṣūm bi-nafsihi*).[17] Since the collapse of the Ottoman Empire until now, the utilization of the Ḥanafī approach has stagnated. Today, many so-called "Islamic" states reject the Ottoman heritage and do not support the *ādamiyyah* paradigm in Islamic law. Instead, they adopt an exclusionist approach to human rights.

The *Ādamiyyah* paradigm went beyond the confines of the Ḥanafī school and gained supporters from other legal schools as well, including Mālikī and Ḥanbalī schools. Many non-Ḥanafī scholars shared the Ḥanafī way of reasoning, such as al-Ghazālī (d. 505/1111) of the Shāfiʿī school, Ibn Taymiyya (d. 728/1328) and Ibn Qayyim al-Jawziyya (d. 751/1350) of the Ḥanbalī school, Ibn Rushd (d. 520/1126), al-Shatibī (d. 790/1388), and Ibn ʿĀshir (d. 1042/1631) of the Mālikī school. As a matter of fact, it would be a mistake to present the *Ādamiyyah* paradigm as specific to the Ḥanafī school only. In fact, the universalist rights discourse transcends the traditional *madhhab* boundaries, even though Abū Ḥanīfa, the eponym of the Ḥanafī school, was the most prominent advocate of this approach.

In this way, a network is developed between Islamic legal traditions based on the universalist discourse. That being said, the universal approach to rights based on *ādamiyyah* has been almost entirely ignored today by those who specialize in human rights in Islam.[18] It is also not implemented by any of the so-called Islamic states. Therefore, there is a need to explore and present the historical foundations of this approach in order to revive it in light of new developments in international, inter-communal, and inter-religious relations.

The reality of globalization, which brings all societies of the world into close interaction, requires Muslims to once again revisit the legal and ethical norms derived from the *Ādamiyyah* paradigm, so they can reshape their relationships with people of other faiths. The legal legacy inherited by Muslims provides a solid universalist approach to rights that they can use today to contribute to human rights developments in the world.

The Justification of Universal Rights

In Islamic thought, the inherent rights that are grounded in one's humanity, referred to as *ḥuqūq al-ādamiyyīn,* are considered inherent and inalienable. These rights are based on the principle that all human beings possess dignity and inviolability by virtue of their creation. As such, these rights are intrinsic to the human condition and can never be lost, because a person can never lose their humanity. This notion ties directly to the Qur'anic understanding that all humans are honored by God and that this honor persists regardless of their actions, beliefs, or societal status. Thus, these inherent rights continue to apply to all individuals as long as they remain human, a condition that is, by definition, immutable.

In Christianity, particularly in classical and Thomistic theology, the idea that humans have universal rights is often grounded in their capacity to know, love, and have a relationship with God. This view posits that because humans are made in the image of God (*imago Dei*), they have an inherent dignity and the potential for communion with God. This capacity for rational thought, moral decision-making, and love of God provides the foundation for their inherent rights.

For instance, Thomas Aquinas argues that humans have a natural inclination to seek God and that this spiritual potential undergirds their moral and legal standing. Thus, the Christian framework can be considered more idealistic because it focuses on the potential of human beings to know and love God. Rights are viewed in terms of their connection to an individual's spiritual journey and ultimate purpose in uniting with God.

Sarakhsī's Justification for Fundamental Rights

Al-Sarakhsī (d. 1090 CE), *Uṣūl al-Sarakhsī**

لأن الله لما خلق الإنسان لحمل أمانته أكرمه بالعقل والذمة ليكون بها أهلا لوجوب حقوق الله عليه. ثم أثبت له العصمة والحرية والملكية ليبقى فيتمكن من أداء ما حمل من الأمانة. ثم هذه الأمانة والحرية والملكية ثابته للمرء من لحظة ولادته، ويكون المميز وغير المميز فيه سواء. فكذلك الذمة الصالحة لوجوب الحقوق فيها ثابت له من حين أن يولد يستوي فيه المميز وغير المميز.

When God created human beings to bear His divine trust, He honored them with intellect and legal capacity, making them eligible for the obligations God placed upon them. He then established for them **inviolability**, **freedom**, and **ownership**, so that they may continue their lives in a manner that enables them to fulfill the responsibility they carry. These rights, inviolability, freedom, and ownership, are inherent in an individual from the moment of birth, and both the discerning and non-discerning are equal in this regard. Thus, the capacity to bear rights and responsibilities is inherent in individuals from birth, and all individuals, regardless of their level of intellectual development, are equal in this respect.

*Al-Sarakhsī, *Uṣūl al-Sarakhsī*, ed. Abū al-Wafā᾽ al-Afghānī, (Beirut: Dār al-Fikr, 2005), vol. 2, 334.

The justification for human rights, as outlined by Al-Sarakhsī, takes a more realistic and pragmatic approach compared the the Christian perspective. In Sarakhsī's view, human beings possess rights not only because of their inherent dignity but because these rights are essential for fulfilling their divine trust (*amānah*) on earth. But more importantly, rights are necessary for human survival itself, which even precedes the ability to carry out one's earthly or otherworldly responsibilities. Without the security of life (*ʿiṣmah*), freedom (*ḥurriyyah*), and ownership (*milkīyyah*), human beings would lack the basic conditions necessary to survive and fulfill their moral and religious obligations.

This perspective recognizes the tangible and practical needs of individuals as part of their divine role in the world. This is a responsibility every human being bears by virtue of being created by God. The rights granted to humans are thus functional and essential for survival, for being able to live in a way that allows them to fulfill their obligations to God and society.

Thus, while Christian thought justifies fundamental rights by emphasizing humanity's higher spiritual potential, the Islamic perspective grounds these rights in the practical and immediate needs required for humans to fulfill their role as *khalīfah* (stewards) of the earth and as responsible beings entrusted with the divine trust (*amānah*). Both frameworks affirm inherent human dignity, but they differ in how they prioritize the justification for universal rights, with Christianity focusing on spiritual potential and Islam emphasizing functional necessity in relation to human purpose and obligations.

The Ibrāhimiyyah Paradigm

"Basic rights are due by virtue of faith and contract of protection."

The social network of the oppositional discourse of the *ibrāhimiyyah* paradigm, or communalist school, had originally emerged from the Shāfiʿī legal tradition. Within this framework, rights are not ascribed to individuals simply by virtue of their humanity but rather through religiously defined categories, such as believers and disbelievers. In this paradigm, legal and social protections are contingent upon faith and contractual agreements with the Islamic state rather than an inherent human status.

Some of the non-Shāfiʿī jurists also advocated this approach. Although al-Shāfiʿī was the first famous advocate of this approach, there were scholars from among the other legal schools who adopted the same approach. The majority of the classical Shīʿī scholars are also among those who have adopted this approach, such as Naṣīr al-Dīn al-Ṭūsī (1201-1274) and al-Muḥaqqiq al-Hillī (c. 1205-1277).

The communalist paradigm is comparable to the civil rights paradigm. Muslim scholars who adopt the idea of citizenship rights generally rely on the following proofs:

- Making war on the disbelievers is a general command in the Qur'an (for example, in verses 9:5 and 8:39);
- Prophet Muhammad ﷺ said: "I have been commanded to fight people until they say 'there is no God but Allah';[19]
- Disbelief, according to the communalist approach, is the greatest sin and cannot be tolerated.

As stated earlier, a universal category of the "human being", comparable to the concept of *ādamiyyah* in Ḥanafī thought, does not exist in Shāfiʿī legal doctrine. Instead, Shāfiʿī legal thought is based on religiously defined categories, such as Muslim and non-Muslim. Muslims are entitled to inviolability by virtue of their belief (*mān*). Non-Muslims, however, are not entitled to inviolability from the outset unless they make a peace agreement with the Islamic state and pay taxes for their security guarantees. The agreement in question is called *dhimmah*, while the paid tax is called *jizyah* or *kharaj,* as mentioned earlier.

According to the Ḥanafī jurists, the *dhimmah* agreement is not the reason for *ʿiṣmah* because inviolability is already universally present in all human beings since birth. This agreement, rather, is an alliance against third parties. According to the Shāfiʿī jurists, on the other hand, being a non-Muslim who is a non-*dhimmī* may be a cause for war. According to the communalist approach, to be a non-Muslim non-citizen means being unprotected. In contrast, according to the Ḥanafī school, non-Muslims are protected by virtue of their inborn human inviolability, even if they are not citizens of an Islamic state. In addition, according to the Shāfiʿī jurists, apostates are punished for their unbelief. Jurists of the Ḥanafī school, however, take the position that apostates can be punished not because of their objection to the veracity of Islam but because it is harmful to society and causes religious confusion. These are some of the issues that stem from the fact that a conception of the universal human being or legally enforced rights is absent in the Shāfiʿī doctrine.

The dominant Shāfiʿī approach, which was also opposed to a significant degree by the majority of scholars from the Māliki, Ḥanbalī and Shīʿī legal schools, has been influential to various degrees in the Arabian Peninsula, Egypt, North Africa, the Iberian Peninsula (Islamic Spain) and Iran, until Ottoman rule. The Zoroastrians, Jews, and Christians residing in these regions lived their lives as *dhimmīs*. They attained inviolability as a result of agreements with Muslim rulers based on the Shāfiʿī doctrine.

We can summarize the critiques of the *ibrāhimiyyah* paradigm as follows. The Qur'anic verses and prophetic narrations that were used as supporting proofs for the communalist position (points 1 and 2), ordering to fight against non-Muslims, are related to times of war or a specific group of polytheistic pagan Arabs in the Arabian Peninsula at that time. Therefore, these commands cannot be generalized.

Against the third-mentioned proof, the argument has been put forth that non-Muslims should be granted the right to learn about Islam. In addition, Islamic law does not punish all sins directed towards God unless they harm other members of society. Moreover, it is forbidden to force anyone to accept Islam. On a more philosophical level, one of the leading Ḥanafī scholars, Burhān al-Dīn al-Marghinānī (d. 1197), criticizes the Shāfiʿī approach as follows:

> "Regarding the proofs of al-Shāfiʿī, we must say that the claim that "the inviolability whose violation causes sin is dependent upon Islam" is unacceptable. The inviolability whose violation causes sin is not related to Islam but to a person. Men were created with the aim to respond to the responsibility imposed on them by the law, but it is clear that

unless injustice and murder are prohibited, a person cannot fulfill his duty. Therefore, the fundamental issue that needs to be protected is the person and related to this subsequently comes the protection of property. In fact, property is not inviolable in and of itself, it is created for the use of humanity and is protected only by taking into account the owner's rights."[20]

In conclusion, the discourse on universal rights in Islamic legal traditions does not center on whether rights are universal, but rather on the extent of their enforceability. The fundamental question is: Is inviolability (*ʿiṣmah*) granted to a person solely by virtue of their humanity (*ādamiyyah*) or is its legal enforcement contingent upon faith and contractual allegiance (*ibrāhimiyyah*)? This debate has shaped centuries of Islamic legal thought and influenced how jurists have conceptualized the role of the state in upholding rights, the jurisdiction of Islamic law, and the obligations of Muslim authorities toward non-Muslims. These questions continue to inform contemporary discussions on human rights, citizenship, and the intersection between legal theory and political governance in modern contexts.

Practical Implications of the Ādamiyyah and Ibrāhimiyyah Paradigms

The supporters of the two competing Islamic legal paradigms we have elaborated upon so far, what I call the *ādamiyyah* and *ibrāhimiyyah* paradigms, have systematically drawn conclusions based on their respective approaches throughout Islamic intellectual history. In many ways, it has shaped and informed key issues in the Islamic legal tradition. In the context of social and international relations, for example, legal scholars interpreted many legal and political issues based on their own paradigmatic approach.

Analyzing all of the implications of this paradigmatic divergence is a very difficult task, which would require a study of the complete classical Islamic legal canon. What we want to do here, however, is to demonstrate some of the extent of the impact of this scholarly disagreement on human rights and communal relations. In order to better illustrate this, we need to look for answers to certain key questions.

De Facto Status of International Relations in Islam

On the international level, the *de facto* status of the relationship between Muslims and non-Muslims is peace, according to the universalist approach. Under normal conditions, non-Muslims are considered friends of Muslims. However, they are considered enemies only if they declare war against Muslims. Hence, the valid reason to start a war can only be a declaration of war against Muslims. In other words, Muslims can make only a "defensive war" in response to an "offensive war" initiated by non-Muslims. In this context, the scholars who adopt the *ādamiyyah* approach carefully draw attention to the distinction between warfare (*ḥarb*) and disbelief (*kufr*). Accordingly, all enemies may be disbelievers, but not all disbelievers are considered enemies.

According to the *ibrāhimiyyah* paradigm, however, the *de facto* status of the relationship between Muslims and non-Muslims who are outside of the jurisdiction of Muslims is the neutrality of war. Under normal circumstances, non-Muslims are defined as potential enemies (*ḥarbī*) and are not considered *de facto* friends to Muslims. The result of this reasoning is that non-Muslims cannot have inviolability by default unless a peace agreement is reached.

Muslim jurists who adopt the *ādamiyyah* paradigm argue that Muslims are obliged to protect the inviolability of all humanity, as all people fall under the protection of Islamic law. Therefore, Muslims are obliged to protect the rights of non-Muslims. As a result, every Muslim individual, group, and state is responsible for all of humankind and is held legally and religiously accountable if they fail.

On the contrary, the Muslim jurists who adopt the *ibrāhimiyyah* paradigm and the civil law perspective argue that Muslims are only obliged to protect the inviolability of their citizens under their jurisdiction. According to this approach, only citizens of an Islamic state fall under the protection of Islam. Muslims are, therefore, not responsible for the protection of the rights of non-Muslims in the absence of any peace agreements. For those non-Muslims who have no peace agreement, the fact of not adhering to the Islamic faith is the most prominent obstacle to having the right to the protection of their basic human rights.

Is Apostasy a Crime?

According to the *ādamiyyah* paradigm, a person cannot be punished merely because he or she became an apostate. This situation is only reversed in the case of treason or damaging the reputation of Islam with premeditated black propaganda. That is unless the person in question causes deliberate confusion and mischief (*fitna*) with the aim of harming the sanctity of the Islamic faith.

The underlying reason for the verse in the Qur'an pertaining to apostasy was a group of hypocrites (*munāfiq*) who pretended to have accepted Islam, only to apostatize from it shortly after, claiming they could not find what they were looking for in the religion, with the sole purpose of deceiving people.[21] As can be understood from this verse, in order to be able to punish apostasy, there must be an activity aimed at destroying Islam. Apostasy that remains at the level of human beliefs and convictions does not require criminal punishment.

The *ādamiyyah* paradigm argues that under normal circumstances non-Muslims cannot be seen as enemies, even if they have renounced Islam through apostasy. On the other hand, the communalist approach is of the opinion that apostasy, as such, is a crime that should be punished. This view is based on the Qur'anic verse without considering the historical condition that caused the revelation of the verse.[22]

Since, according to the *ibrāhimiyyah* paradigm, citizenship is based on faith, people who lose their religion and apostate from Islam also lose their rights as citizens. Accordingly, the apostate who lost the right to inviolability is regarded as an enemy who has committed treason, since he is a non-Muslim and no longer a citizen of the Islamic state.

Another point that needs to be mentioned in order to clarify the issue is that Islamic law does not punish a woman who rejects or apostates from Islam under any circumstances. There is consensus among all Muslim jurists from all schools that the punishment for apostasy is not applied to women. In addition, due to the Prophet Muhammad's ﷺ strict prohibition, legal scholars agreed that non-Muslim women should not be killed during the war.

The Ḥanafī scholars drew attention to this point of consensus regarding the practice of not killing women during the war to support their legal position. If the reason for punishing apostasy was leaving the religion, women and men would be punished in the same way. According to the scholars of the Ḥanafī school, therefore, it is not apostasy alone, but also betrayal and getting involved in an offensive war against Muslims is an act that requires criminal sanction.

Punishment and Losing Inviolability

This topic concerns the legal and ethical status of criminals and convicts within Islamic law. Across all major Islamic legal schools, a mere accusation does not lead to the loss of a person's inviolability (*ʿiṣmah*). There is unanimous agreement among master jurists (*mujtahidūn*) that an accused individual retains full human rights until guilt is established through due legal process. Only after a conviction can punitive measures be applied in accordance with Islamic law.

Among the legal schools, Ḥanafī jurists adopt a particularly cautious stance. They generally prohibit the combination of punishment and financial compensation for a single offense. In their view, a convict may be subjected either to corporal punishment or to financial restitution, but not both simultaneously. In contrast, Shāfiʿī scholars permit both punishment and compensation in certain cases, such as theft, where a thief may be penalized and also required to return stolen property or pay restitution.

The preceding examples illustrate how varying interpretations of human inviolability (*ʿiṣmah*) are reflected in legal practice. Diverging paradigms concerning the foundation of rights have led to distinct legal outcomes across the Islamic legal tradition. All paradigms affirm the principle of *ʿiṣmah*, yet they differ in the extent to which the state is obligated to enforce or protect this inviolability in specific contexts. In this light, examining the interpretive variation between the *ādamiyyah* and *ibrāhīmiyyah* paradigms helps illuminate the diversity of legal approaches within Islamic jurisprudence without suggesting a fundamental rupture in the underlying moral framework.

Notes

1. The Islamic calendar starts from the migration (*hijra*) of Prophet Muhammad ﷺ from Makkah to Medina in the year 622 and is typically referred to in English as Anno Hegirae (abbreviated as AH). The first century AH corresponds to the seventh century of the internationally used Gregorian calendar, which originated in the Christian West.
2. See Tareq Sharawi, "How Does Islam Treat People Outside of the Abrahamic Religions? Between Ādamiyya and Ibrāhīmiyya" (PhD diss., Ibn Haldun University, 2020).
3. Muslim jurists historically divided the world into two realms: lands that properly belonged to the Islamic community and were ruled by the Islamic sacred law (*sharīʿa*) and lands that were under the rulership of non-Muslims. The first is called the "Abode of Islam" (*dār al-islām*) while the second is called the "Abode of War" (*dār al-ḥarb*).
4. See, for example Burhān al-Dīn Al-Marghinānī. *Al-Hidāyah fi Sharḥ Bidāyah al-Mubtadī* I-IV, (eds. Muḥammad Muḥammad Tamir, Hafiz ʿĀshur Hafiz), Cairo: Dār al-Salām 1420/2000), 22: 852; Badr al-Din al-ʿAyni (855 / 1451), *al-Bināyah fī Sharḥ al-Hidāyah*, ed. Muḥammad Omar (Beirut: Dār al-Fikr, 1980 / 1400), 5:830-831; ʿAlāʾ al-Dīn al-Kāsānī. *Badāʾiʿ al-Ṣanāʾiʿ fī Tartīb al-Sharāʾiʿ*, Beirut: Dār al-Fikr 1406/1986), VII: 233-241.
5. Al-Dabūsī, Abū Zayd ʿAbd Allāh ibn ʿUmar. *Taqwīm al-Adilla fī Uṣūl al-Fiqh*. Edited by Khalīl Muḥyī al-Dīn al-Mays. (Beirut: Dār al-Kutub al-ʿIlmiyyah, 2001), p. 417.
6. Muḥammad al-Sarakhsī, *Usūl al-Sarakhsī*, vol.2 (India: Lajnat Iḥyāʾ al-Maʿārif al-Nuʿmāniyyah, 1395 AH/1976 CE), 334.
7. See Ibn Māza, *al-Muḥīṭ al-Burhānī fī al-Fiqh al-Nuʿmānī*.
8. Fakhr al-Dīn al-Zaylaʿī, *Tabyīn al-Ḥaqāʾq*, vol. 4 (DKI: Dār al-Kutub al-ʿilmiyyah, 2010), 139.
9. Muḥammad Amīn ibn ʿĀbdīn, *Radd al-Muḥtār*, vol.7 (DKI: Dār al-Kutub al-ʿilmiyyah, 2011), 245.
10. Qur'an 2:193. All English renderings of Qur'anic verses are taken from the translation of M. H. S. Abdel Haleem, *The Qur'an* (New York: Oxford University Press, 2010).
11. "*There is no compulsion in religion: true guidance has become distinct from error, so whoever rejects false gods and believes in God has grasped the firmest hand-hold, one that will never break. God is all hearing and all knowing.*" (Qurʿan 2:256)

12. Therefore, the following principle is put forth: "*The human being is honored according to Islamic law, even if they are a disbeliever.*" (Arabic: *al-adamī mukarram shar'an wa law kāfiran*), see Muḥammad Amin Ibn 'Abidin, *Radd al-muḥtār 'alā al-durr al-mukhtār (*Istanbul: Kahraman Yay. 1984), 5:58. Ibn 'Abidin also mentioned that this principle conflicts with the idea of slavery.
13. "*Do not take life, which God has made sacred, except by right: if anyone is killed wrongfully, We have given authority to the defender of his rights, but he should not be excessive in taking life, for he is already aided [by God].*" (Qur'an 17:33) "*You who believe, be steadfast in your devotion to God and bear witness impartially: do not let hatred of others lead you away from justice, but adhere to justice, for that is closer to awareness of God. Be mindful of God: God is well aware of all that you do.*" (Qur'an 5:8) "[…] if anyone kills a person, unless in retribution for murder or spreading corruption in the land – it is as if he kills all mankind, while if any saves a life it is as if he saves the lives of all mankind." (Qur'an 5:32) In the address which the Prophet ﷺ delivered on the occasion of the Farewell Hajj, he said: "Your lives and properties are forbidden to one another till you meet your Lord on the Day of Resurrection." The Prophet ﷺ has also said about the dhimmīs (the non-Muslim citizens of the Muslim state): "*One who kills a man under covenant (i.e., dhimmī) will not even smell the fragrance of Paradise.*" (See Recep Şentürk, "Veda Hutbelerinde İnsan Hakları" in *Hz. Peygamberin Veda Haccı Hutbeleri Sempozyum Tebliğleri* 2-3 Kasım 2019 (ed. Suat Mertoğlu), Ankara: Diyanet İşleri Başkanlığı, 2021.
14. 'Amr b. al-'Ās was a companion of the Prophet Muhammad ﷺ who played a major role in the later conquests of Egypt, Syria, and Palestine. He also served as a governor of some of these areas.
15. The Mughal rulers of India banned the *sati* tradition but were unable to completely banish it. See Sri Ram Sharma, *The Religious Policy of the Mughal Emperors* (Una, Himachal Pradesh: Asia Publishing House, 1972), 42-44; Zulfaqar Mubed, *Hinduism During the Mughal India of the 17th Century*, trans. David Shea and Anthony Troyer (Patna: Khuda Bakhsh Oriental Public Library, 1993, originally published in 1843), 77.
16. The *millet* system was a form of diversity management in which the Ottoman state allowed adherents of other faiths a great amount of autonomy. For example, Christians and Jews, to a large degree, were allowed to govern their respective communities according to their own religious laws. It has been a primary historical example of religious pluralism.
17. 'Abd al-Ghanī al-Maydānī, *al-Lubāb fi Sharḥ al-Kitāb*, (Cairo: No publisher,, 1383 / 1963), IV:128.

18. For a brief discussion in Arabic scholarship on the human rights discourse in Islam, see Salma al-Khadra al-Jayyusi, ed., *Ḥuqūq al-Insān fī al-Fikr al-ʿArabī* (Beirut: Markaz Dirāsāt al-Waḥda al-ʿArabiyya, 2002). There is no significant mention of the universalist Ḥanafī approach in this book.
19. *Ṣaḥīḥ Muslim 21b Book 1, Hadith 34.*
20. This is an intentional citation by way of example from an earlier English translation of the book. Burhān al-Dīn al-Marghinānī, *The Hedaya or Guide: a Commentary on the Mussulman Laws* (tr. Charles Hamilton) (Karachi: Daru'l-Ishaat, 1989) II, 201-2.
21. "*Some of the People of the Book say, 'At the beginning of the day, believe in what has been revealed to these believers [the Muslims], then at the end of the day reject it, so that they too may turn back, but do not sincerely believe in anyone unless he follows your own religion'- [Prophet], tell them, 'True guidance is the guidance of God'- [they say], 'Do not believe that anyone else could be given a revelation similar to what you were given, or that they could use it to argue against you in your Lord's presence.' [Prophet], tell them, 'All grace is in God's hands: He grants it to whoever He will- He is all embracing, all knowing.*" (Qur'an 3:72-78)
22. "*As for those who believe, then reject the faith, then believe again, then reject the faith again and become increasingly defiant, God will not forgive them, nor will He guide them on any path.*" (Qur'an 4:137); "*They swear by God that they did not, but they certainly did speak words of defiance and became defiant after having submitted; they tried to do something, though they did not achieve it, —being spiteful was their only response to God and His Messenger enriching them out of His bounty. They would be better off turning back [to God]: if they turn away, God will punish them in this world and the Hereafter, and there will be no one on earth to protect or help them.*" (Qur'an 9:74); "*Then there are those who built a mosque—in an attempt to cause harm, disbelief, and disunity among the believers—as an outpost for those who fought God and His Messenger before: they swear, 'Our intentions were nothing but good,' but God bears witness that they are liars.*" (Qur'an 9:107)

CHAPTER FOUR

Why Did Muslim Scholars Approach the Universality of Rights Differently?

All Muslim legal scholars recognized the importance of rights, but some placed greater emphasis on their universality and full inclusivity than others. However, the disagreement was not about whether rights are universal, but rather about their universal enforceability. This distinction leads us to two key explanatory questions: Why did all scholars of classical Islamic jurisprudence emphasize rights? Why did some Muslim jurists disagree on the universal enforceability of rights?

The first question highlights the consensus among Islamic jurists that rights are a foundational concern in Islamic law. The second question points to the juridical divergence regarding who holds the authority to enforce these rights and under what conditions. These differences stem from varying interpretations of scriptural sources (*naṣṣ*), legal reasoning (*ijtihād*), and historical considerations related to governance, political authority, and jurisdictional boundaries.

The answer to the first question lies in the relationship between religious scholars (*ʿulamāʾ*) and the state, which has historically shaped the development of Islamic jurisprudence and the autonomy of legal interpretation. The answer to the second question stems from the diverse methodological approaches Muslim jurists adopted, leading to differing perspectives on the scope and enforceability of rights.

Religious Scholars and the State

All Islamic legal schools have opposed historical efforts by Muslim rulers to canonize Islamic law. This goes against the legal diversity of the Islamic legal tradition, and Muslims are free to accept or follow any school or legal interpretation (*ijtihād*) they wish. Muslim jurists thought that legal canonization would lead to a monopoly in law or religious interpretation and would increase the pressure of the state on society.

For this reason, Islamic law has never been a positive law or official state law throughout Islamic history. Hence, the religious law of Muslims never resembled the canon law of the Christian church. And it was only very seldom canonized by state decree. It was only towards the end of the nineteenth century that the Ottomans canonized Islamic law in the *Mecelle*, which served as a civil code for commercial law throughout the late Ottoman Empire.[1]

Muslim scholars stressed that their words are not divine. No human doctrine can truly embrace the absolute will of God. Qualified and well-trained legal scholars interpret the will of Allah through various methods of legal reasoning (*ijtihād*). For this reason, master jurists (*mujtahid*) have clarified that while their legal interpretation is based on divine law, it is still the product of their human intellect.

As the Islamic legal historian Baber Johansen pointed out, Islamic epistemology is characterized by freedom of expression and freedom of religion.[2] Some legal scholars have expressed this reality as follows: "While I know I am right I may have made a mistake, and while I know that the opposite view is wrong, it may also be right."

Therefore, master jurists put limits on their authority despite all the incentives of the state. Also, according to the scholarly consensus, imitation in faith (*taqlīd*) cannot be accepted. Every Muslim is obliged to strengthen his or her faith by using their intellect. Blind faith is rejected. For this reason, when someone asks, "why are you Muslim?" the answer cannot be "because the society I live in, my family or scholars have said that this is the right way". Even if one cannot convince everybody, one has to rely on evidence to convince oneself. On the other hand, in matters of law and morality, one is free to follow a qualified master jurist of their choice, as these issues are not as fundamental as faith. Additionally, it is not possible for everyone to specialize in law and moral issues.

None of the founders of the four legal schools accepted the proposals made to them by rulers to serve at the top levels of the administration. It is worth considering, therefore, if this firm relationship between scholars and the state had an effect on the development of the theory of inviolability (*ʿiṣmah*).

Abū Ḥanīfa, whom the Abbasid administration wanted to assign as the chief judge, did not accept the offer despite the torture he experienced during his later years. His behavior can be considered an example of civil disobedience. Whether the personal experience of Abū Ḥanīfa regarding the state had an influence on his emphasis on universal human rights and freedom of the individual is an unanswered question. Similarly, Imām Mālik refused when the Abbasid caliph requested permission to canonize his legal work *al-Muwatta'* for use everywhere in the Islamic state. He did this so as not to limit the understanding of Islamic law by adhering to the interpretation of a single person.[3]

Aḥmad ibn Ḥanbal was among the notable Muslim scholars who faced persecution under the Abbasid regime for refusing to endorse the state's official theological position. Similarly, Imām al-Shāfiʿī, who studied under both Aḥmad ibn Ḥanbal and Muḥammad al-Shaybānī, declined state appointments and chose to sustain himself through his own means rather than become financially dependent on the ruling authorities.

Some scholars interpret this historical pattern as an Islamic mechanism for regulating the relationship between political authority and religious scholarship. It represents a conscious effort to define the distinct roles of rulers and the *ʿulamāʾ* and ensure that legislative authority remained in the hands of scholars rather than the state. In doing so, Islamic civilization avoided concentrating all forms of power in the hands of the state.

Had the religious scholars submitted to political pressures and allowed their legal interpretations to be formalized and codified by state authority, Islam might have developed a centralized religious institution capable of monopolizing the definition of right and wrong, lawful and unlawful.[4] However, the master jurists were bound to religious consciousness (*taqwā*) and perceived it as a disgrace to be appointed as an employee by the state. Hence, they used the famous expression: "*The worst scholars frequent the houses of the rulers while the best rulers frequent the houses of the scholars.*"[5]

Distancing themselves from bureaucratic positions in the government gave Muslim jurists a great amount of autonomy. The rejection of proposals that other people would have desired and kept away from state corruption and oppression increased the authority and legitimacy Muslim scholars enjoyed in society. It is thus apparent that the scholars of Islam aimed to win the hearts and minds of the people by rejecting state power.

The rulers, who generally had relatively less piety and less impact on society, cooperated with the scholars of their time. The relations, however, did not always go smoothly. Some scholars accepted official duties for the effective implementation of Islamic law through state sanctions. But resistance continued. For example, the religious seminary (*madrasa*) or university was relatively more integrated with the official system, while Sufi lodges and religious orders rejected it. Ascetic and Sufi scholars preferred to remain relatively more independent of worldly powers. Even the *madrasa* scholars received their wages not from the state but from the resources of private foundations (*waqf*) that were established to support education.

In the Ottoman hierarchy, the S*haykh al-Islam* often came before the grand vizier.[6] The *Shaykh al-Islam* was the only person in the Sublime Port to have the authority to revoke government decisions and was the second authority after the Ottoman sultan. However, the scholars were not strictly organized or unified under a single authority.

The Islamic scholarly class differed from the Christian clergy. It was organized in a more informal and organic way compared to the Christian church structure. Hence, scholars acted as individual authorities linked to each other through an informal and intellectual social network formed by close relations with various schools of thought. At the same time, the Islamic state generally developed as a well-organized structure from the inception of Islamic history, notwithstanding several instances of civil strife.

Ultimately, the representation of religion fell under the authority of individual scholars. Only they had the sole capacity to raise students to the rank of a scholar. Hence, they hold significant authority. Not even the state had the authority to certify scholars (*ijāzah*). Similarly, it was not a state institution but only scholars who had the jurisdiction to pronounce religious legal verdicts on matters. Intellectuals need government protection to freely express and implement their ideas. The Muslim scholars can be considered to have supported the theory of human rights in order to guarantee everyone's protection, including that of themselves, against powerful actors in society and especially the state.

By the same token, Abū Ḥanīfa's personal relationship with the state, as a migrant and member of the merchant class, may have influenced his remarkably inclusive approach towards rights and individual freedom. Not only was he an important scholar, but he was also a merchant, especially during his youth. In addition, he was from the second generation to enter Islam.

While the founders of the other legal schools also faced oppression, they did not face the difficulties he was confronted with as a merchant, convert and immigrant. These factors may, to some extent, shed light on why Abū Ḥanīfa so strongly supported universal human rights, whether deliberately or not.

Notes

1. The *Mecelle* (called the *Majallah al-Aḥkām al-ʿAdliyyah* in Arabic) remained part of the law of many countries that formerly belonged to the Ottoman Empire, such as Jordan, Iraq, and Palestine.
2. Baber Johansen, *Contingency in a Sacred Law: Legal and Ethical Norms in the Muslim Fiqh* (Leiden: Brill, 1999), 238-262.
3. See Samy Ayoub, "The Mecelle, Sharia, and the Ottoman State: Fashioning and Refashioning of Islamic Law in the Nineteenth and Twentieth Centuries," *Journal of the Ottoman and Turkish Studies Association* 2, no. 1 (2015): 121-146.
4. For more on canonization, see Ahmed El Shamsy, *The Canonization of Islamic Law: A Social and Intellectual History* (New York: Cambridge University Press, 2013).
5. See, for example, Abū Ḥāmid al-Ghazālī, *The Book of Knowledge*, trans. Kenneth Honerkamp (Fons Vitae, 2016).
6. In the Ottoman political system, the *Shaykh al-Islam* was the highest-ranking religious authority while the grand vizier was the effective head of state.

CHAPTER FIVE

Minority Rights in the Islamic Legal Tradition

Until the nineteenth century, at least a dozen religious legal traditions co-existed in the Ottoman Empire: five non-Muslim (Jewish, Armenian, Orthodox, Catholic, Coptic), four Sunnī (Mālikī, Shāfi'ī, Ḥanbalī, Ḥanafī) and many Shī'ī (such as the Zaydī and Ja'farī). During the second half of the nineteenth century, under European influence, secular law was also added to the Ottoman legal tradition (for instance, international commercial courts). Each religious community promulgated and enforced its own private law, thereby contributing to the diversity of legal discourse. The state did not produce any of these laws itself, nor did it accept any of them as the only official law of the state. Instead, Muslims and non-Muslims produced their own laws. The state treated them all equally and respected each of them. This is called "legal pluralism."

In contrast, in the late nineteenth and early twentieth centuries, which was a period of intense modernization, only one official law was applied in the empire. The first Ottoman constitution was declared on December 23, 1876. With this constitution, the Ottoman Empire became perhaps the first Muslim country to have a constitution.

After the general election for the first time in the history of Islam, the Ottoman parliament convened in March 1877 following the constitution. The parliament attempted to make Islamic law the official state law throughout the empire. This was the first time Islamic law was issued by the state, which marked the end of the traditional pluralist legal system.

One of the reasons for Ottoman political and legal reforms, which were partly imitating European intellectual trends, was the need for a unified legal system due to the centralization and growth of the bureaucracy in the nineteenth century. Eventually, the general application of Islamic law in the Ottoman Empire was a short-lived experience. After the fall of the Ottoman Empire, the Republic of Turkey was established, which went even further in the Westernization process by adopting a fully secular legal system. During this period, a process was initiated that resulted in a mixture of translated legal rules from many different Western countries.[1]

In every stage of this process, the identity and rights of minorities have been redefined as a result of the reshaping of the relationship between law and religion to facilitate greater control over society by the state. In retrospect, we see that this strategy failed with many unforeseen dire consequences.

When analyzing the Islamic Ottoman and secular Turkish experience, we can divide minority rights in Islamic law into three stages:

- The classical age, from the seventh to the late eighth century.
- The period of Islamic modernization, from the nineteenth century to the first quarter of the twentieth century.

- The period of secularization or separation of law and religion, from the first quarter of the twentieth century to the present day.

This broad and imprecise periodization stems from the specific history of the Ottoman Empire and the Republic of Turkey and its unique experience of secularization.

The Islamic Legal Tradition

The Islamic legal tradition will be better understood if seen as part of the Western legal tradition, just as historians of religions have studied the Islamic religion as a Western religion. In fact, as Richard Bulliet demonstrated, since the Middle Ages, the histories of Europe and the Muslim world have been intertwined, and the great transformations in the Islamic and European legal traditions show striking parallels at all stages.[2]

Both Muslims and non-Muslims enjoy remarkable freedom under classical Islamic law. This reality brought about a state of legal pluralism that accommodates Muslims and non-Muslims from different perspectives. This phenomenon could be defined as an "open law," which means a legal system that peacefully co-exists with many legal systems and discourse communities in one society and protects them. In this period, the dominant principle was: "*One legal interpretation (ijtihād) cannot override another.*"

Every religious community under Islamic rule had considerable autonomy so that it could regulate its internal affairs according to its traditional law. Besides Jews and Christians, this right was granted to all religious communities, including Pagans, Buddhists, Hindus, Zoroastrians, and Sabaeans. To show their close connection to Islam, Jews and Christians were called the People of the Book (*Ahl al-Kitāb*).

It is a common misunderstanding that Islamic law gives freedom of religion only to those who belong to the People of the Book. A brief review of classical Islamic legal texts, especially as they were implemented in Iran and the Indian Subcontinent, proves that the opposite of this claim is true. Moreover, each Islamic school of law had the right to practice Islam according to their own interpretation. As new discourse communities emerged among Muslims and non-Muslims, the "open law" approach allowed them to join the pluralist legal system under Islamic rules.

Among those who compared Islamic law in terms of minority rights in Muslim and non-Muslim societies throughout the Middle Ages, there were those who found Islamic law progressive. In a democratic and pluralistic system, the question of whether Islam gives equal rights to minorities or whether they can be recognized today is related to a broader debate about the relationship between religion and law. Can any religion do this?

The moral and legal legitimation of minorities is a prerequisite for the protection of sustainable minority rights in a pluralistic and democratic government. Today, such a legitimation is provided either by a secular ideology or religion, despite the great difference between religious and secular perspectives.

The most prevalent view in secularist circles is that religion cannot protect or respect minority rights, because these rights can only be guaranteed from a non-religious or secular point of view. The fact that most religions have been abused to justify the oppression of religious minorities supports this claim. Moreover, religion has also been abused to justify the oppression of women, racial minorities and colonized people.

The moral and legal legitimation of minorities is a prerequisite for the protection of sustainable minority rights in a pluralistic and democratic government. Today, such a legitimation is provided either by a secular ideology or religion, despite the great difference between religious and secular perspectives.

The most prevalent view in secularist circles is that religion cannot protect or respect minority rights, because these rights can only be guaranteed from a non-religious or secular point of view. The fact that most religions have been abused to justify the oppression of religious minorities supports this claim. Moreover, religion has also been abused to justify the oppression of women, racial minorities and colonized people. However, this view suffers from being one-sided. History shows that religions have also contributed to the liberation of minorities, even if perhaps not to its full extent. For example, Christian and Muslim religious leaders led the civil rights movement in America. Jews fleeing from Spain were given shelter in Istanbul by the caliph.

In contrast, secular ideologies, such as nationalism and communism, have also been used by some of their supporters to justify the oppression of minorities. Hence, there is a complex relationship between particular cultures, religious or secular, and respect or apathy for minority rights. Clarifying the relationship between the two requires a balanced, comprehensive, and cautious approach. Islamic law can be used as an example to demonstrate that secular (rational) and religious modes of legal reasoning are not mutually exclusive. In other words, secular and religious perspectives substantiate each other if properly combined through a multiplex epistemology and methodology.[3]

In Islamic law, minority rights were established on the basis of the principle of humanity (*ādamiyyah*). The principle of humanity makes it possible for people to have the right to legal personality (*dhimmah*), which requires the right to inviolability.

Islamic Law and Minority Rights

Islamic law approaches minority rights at two levels: the level of the individual and the level of society. An individual member of a minority group is called a *dhimmī,* and a minority community is called a *millah* (*millet* in Turkish). While a *dhimmī* is defined as a person with legal responsibility and inviolability, a *millah* is a religious community or a community united around a religious identity, practice, and discourse. At both levels, human rights and constitutional or legal rights are granted to minorities.

Human rights are universal and, therefore, do not change from person to person or from community to community. Constitutional or legal rights, however, can vary from group to group or from person to person. Regardless of how autonomous an individual is, he or she is almost viewed within a certain social network when it comes to addressing and determining rights and duties. An emphasis on humanity (*ādamiyyah*) can be seen as an emphasis on personal autonomy. After the Ottoman reforms, the traditional *millet* system was abandoned, and an attempt was made towards comprehensive Islamic reforms that took equal citizenship for all individuals, and not religious communities, as a basis for its relationship with political authority.

Muslim jurists have put forward different views on why minorities should be given rights. The main source of discussion between scholars was the question of whether rights should be granted to minorities because of their humanity or citizenship. Classical and modern Muslim jurists have defended diverse opinions in this regard.

The divergence between universalist and communalist conceptions of rights is evident across all major legal traditions, including Islamic law. The universalist approach asserts that rights are inherent to all human beings by virtue of their humanity (*ādamiyyah*), irrespective of their religious, ethnic, or national affiliation. Hence, it defends equal rights for all people, regardless of class, race, color, language, religion, ethnicity or any other inherited and inherent characteristics. As mentioned above, this view was formulated by Ḥanafī scholars and found its expression in the basic principle: "*Inviolability is the right of all people by virtue of their humanity.*"

In contrast, the communalist approach restricts rights to members of a specific political or social community defined by citizenship. The communalist school does not accept universally granted human rights. Instead, it defends civil rights or constitutional rights granted to citizens because of their citizenship. This view is expressed in the basic principle: "*Inviolability is a right that is established by faith or through an agreement for protection.*" This fundamental distinction shapes legal and ethical debates on justice, inclusion, and the scope of legal protections in different historical and contemporary contexts.

A similar tension is observed in the history of Western law. The sixth article of the United Nations Universal Declaration of Human Rights states that: "*Everybody has the right to be recognized as an individual before the law everywhere.*" This sentence should be seen as the result of long discussions and disagreements within human history. Before this declaration, some segments of the population in the West, especially blacks, women, minorities and non-citizens, did not have the right to "legal personality." The right to legal personality brings human rights and responsibilities along with it. Without a legal personality, people cannot have rights and duties. In this case, they are not considered as people with moral capacity but merely as goods or outcasts.

In some periods of Western history, the rejection of the right to legal personality meant that they were not accepted as human beings. In this context, the discrimination of colonized people, Afro-Americans before the civil rights movement in America, Jews before Jewish freedom in Europe, and women until the twentieth century are well-known examples. The sixth article of the UN Declaration aimed to end such discriminatory practices.

Personal Rights in Islam

Personal rights are of central importance to understanding the concept of minority rights. As mentioned earlier, the word *dhimmah* in classical Islamic law means legal responsibility and inviolability, which is often called legal personality in modern legal discourse. Moral, religious, and legal responsibility requires a person to have *dhimmah*.

If a person possesses *dhimmah*, he or she can have rights and responsibilities. *Dhimmah* separates people from animals because people are responsible for their actions. Hence, to have *dhimmah* gives someone the right to be a full member of society. Legal responsibility before the law is a prerequisite for community membership, which brings the right to inviolability.

Dhimmah is also commonly understood as protection, agreement (*ʿahd*) and peace (*ṣulḥ*), because this is an agreement that subsumes non-Muslims under Muslim protection. Therefore, the expression "this falls under his or her *dhimmah*" means that a person is responsible before the law or is protected under the law. This legal responsibility may be in the form of a written agreement or a general law.

Related to this issue, there is a conceptual discussion between the universalists and communalists about who has *dhimmah* and on what basis. This scholarly debate divided Muslim jurists into two groups. Some Muslim jurists argue that *dhimmah* is an innate right and that every person has it once he or she is created in the mother's womb. Others claim that *dhimmah* is an acquired right and that people obtain it because of their citizenship. While non-Muslim individuals with personal rights are called *dhimmī*, their community as a whole is called *ahl al-dhimmah*, which means "people with legal responsibility and inviolability."

According to Muslim jurists of the universalist school, all people have *dhimmah* merely by virtue of being human. Therefore, the term *ahl al-dhimmah,* in its literal sense, applies to all individuals, as everyone is born with *dhimmah.* In this context, *dhimmah* can be called an innate right or a natural right. Consequently, non-Muslim minorities also have legal personality and legal responsibilities by default. Thus, the *dhimmah* compact can be seen as a declaration of equality between Muslims and non-Muslims.

Other non-Muslims who have not yet made an agreement with the Muslim state authority must also officially declare and record their legal responsibility before the law. From this point of view, the *dhimmah* agreement is only a process that demonstrates the declaration of mutual rights and duties by both parties. Signing the *dhimmah* agreement with Muslims will not give non-Muslims new rights, since non-Muslims already have these rights by virtue of their humanity.

At the level of positive legal or constitutional rights, the universalist school permits diversity and accepts differences between Muslims and non-Muslims. This diversity is apparent in the cases of interreligious marriage, inheritance, and testimony against criminal suspects from other religions. In addition, non-Muslims are not required to do military service or serve the state, which can be considered either an advantage or a restriction. Nevertheless, there is also a clear restriction, which is that a non-Muslim cannot be the head of an Islamic state. Non-Muslims can occupy all positions except that of state leadership.

The communalists do not share the views of the universalists on this matter. They hold that *dhimmah* is a status that only Muslims can enjoy, and that non-Muslims only achieve this status through an agreement with Muslims. From this point of view, *dhimmah* is an acquired right and privilege. This is also the ground for other rights that can be gained by signing an agreement with the Muslim authority. Having a legal personality requires meeting the terms of the agreement. Otherwise, this right may be lost. One of the conditions for having a legal personality is to pay a special "head tax" to the state (i.e., paying *jizyah*).[4]

From the communalist point of view, *jizyah* is a tax paid in exchange for *dhimmah*, which grants a person inviolability and the right to settle (*suknā*) in the Islamic state. But the universalists argue the opposite. According to them, *dhimmah* and *ʿiṣmah* are not the subject of monetary exchange; rather, they are inherent and irreversible universal rights. From this perspective, just as Muslims must pay *zakāt* and other annual charity and taxes, non-Muslims must pay taxes under the name *jizyah*.

According to the Ḥanafī school, *jizyah* can be collected from all non-Muslims, including the people of the book (*ahl al-kitāb*) and non-Arab pagans, with the only exception of Arabs who worshiped idols. According to the Shāfiʿī school, *jizyah* can only be collected from the people of the book (*ahl al-kitāb*) and Zoroastrians. It is not collected from members of other religions because the Qur'an and *ḥadīth* do not count them among those who are allowed to sign peace agreements with Muslims.

The Mughal state in India and the Ottomans, who were following the Ḥanafī school, collected *jizyah* from all religious members without distinguishing them. Among the non-Muslim subjects, only the capable, young, healthy, and working male adults were obliged to pay *jizyah*. Non-Muslim women, children, the elderly, the sick, the unemployed, the disabled, and clergy were not obliged to do so.

Community Rights for Minorities in Islamic Law

Islamic law recognizes two large groups, the Muslim community and the non-Muslim community, each with its own subdivisions. The Muslim community is divided into two large groups, Shīʿa and Sunnī, each divided into various schools of law (*madhhab*). Subgroups of Muslims are called communities (*millah*). The institutional organization in which all these groups are linked horizontally with each other and vertically with the Muslim ruler is called the *millah* system.

The pluralistic social and legal system is based on a certain normative facts approach, which makes it possible for different communities and schools of thought to co-exist in a particular society. From the outset, Islamic law accepted that normative social reality is plural rather than uniform and monolithic. There is a consensus that this is the case at the social level. The disagreement is about whether normative social reality is plural in God's sight: Does God allow people to adopt different normative rules, although He knows that only one of these sets of rules is valid? Or does He accept as valid all normative rules adopted by people? Can these diverse norms be valid in God's sight if they are supported by rational proofs and evidence from sacred texts?

The answer to these questions can never be known or evaluated. Even those who admit that normative social reality is only one in the sight of God verify that He allows for the normative social reality to be diverse and heterogeneous in human society and, therefore, will not blame those who fail to know reality with certainty.

Prophet Muhammad ﷺ said:

> While Allah gives two rewards to a legal scholar who is right in his legal reasoning and decision (*ijtihād*), he gives only one reward to the legal scholar who is wrong in his legal reasoning and decision, although he has good intention.[5]

What is important here, if the limitation of the human intellect is taken into account, is the serious and sincere effort to find what is right and wrong. In all of these discussions, classical Muslim jurists have acknowledged that God allows the normative reality to be plural at the social level.

Islamic jurists also acknowledged that Muslims are not the only representatives of normative truth. Secular and religious reasoning, whether carried out by Muslims or non-Muslims can lead one to a normative truth. Muʿtazilī scholars argued that human beings have the rational powers to discover what is right and wrong in every subject. According to them, the role of divine revelation is to justify what people can rationally discover by using their intellects.

On the other hand, most of the legal scholars belonging to the Sunnī and Shīʿa schools agree that humans are not able to differentiate between right and wrong solely through the intellect. They also maintain that what we learn of what is right and wrong from divine books and prophets is in accordance with our intellect.

Moreover, Islamic law, which empowers minorities in their own legal practice, recognizes the social legitimacy of pre-Islamic religions within certain rules. Muslim scholars acknowledge that all divine- or heavenly-inspired religions are from God and that their members worship the same God. God's religion is one, but this religion has been sent to every nation in their own language because Allah never punishes a society without sending a prophet who speaks in their language. From this point of view, all religions are previous forms of the religion of God, which retains its authentic form to varying degrees. Islam came to verify the messages of these previous religions and to correct the corrupted ones, not to falsify them. According to this approach, the superiority of Islam is because it is Allah's last message to humanity:

> The [Muslim] believers, the Jews, the Christians, and the Sabians - all those who believe in God and the Last Day and do good - will have their rewards with their Lord. No fear for them, nor will they grieve. (Qur'an 2:62)

Based on this view of other religions, Muslim legal scholars acknowledge that the law of previous religions may also serve as a source for Islamic law when there is an issue that Islamic sacred scripture does not respond to.

This principle is commonly known as "the *sharīʿa* of those who came before us" (*sharʿu mā qablanā*). This goes beyond simply allowing the existence or enforcement of non-Muslim traditional law, because it also opens the door to exchanging of ideas, social relationships, and constructive interaction. From this perspective, truth is shared by all social groups and cannot be monopolized by a particular group or ruling class. Accepting normativity as a multilayered system reduces the social and cultural tensions brought about by different interpretations of reality. It also prevents values, beliefs, and thoughts from turning into social and political conflicts.[6]

Muslim Minorities

The literature investigating minorities under Muslim rule ignores the principle of a "multilayered and plural normative reality," which is the basis of the Islamic approach to minorities. This is especially the case when it comes to examining non-Muslims and the *millet* system. If we really want to understand the whole Islamic framework with regard to minorities, we should include in our study not only non-Muslim minorities but also Muslim minorities.

How were Muslim minorities, differing from the majority in terms of ethnicity, language, or school of thought, treated by the majority? Muslim minorities were organized in Muslim societies primarily in the form of two civil organizations: schools of thought (*madhhab*) and Sufi orders (*ṭarīqah*). During the Umayyad period (661-750), the relationship between Arabs and non-Arabs was problematic due to the official state ideology based on Arab superiority (*shuʿūbiyyah*).

There was also the experience of a period of fierce oppression which was known as the *Mihna* (833-848).[7] During this time, the Abbasid state not only accepted the Muʿtazilite doctrine but also pressured all other scholars to subscribe to this particular theological view. Similarly, there were times when some of the Sufis were oppressed because of their belief in the oneness of being (*waḥdat al-wujūd*), the best example of which was the life and execution of the famous Sufi al-Hallaj (d. 309 AH / 922 CE). These are some of the rare historical examples that show what can happen if Islamic law is not fully implemented.

As a result of the Islamic pluralist approach, most of the Muslim and non-Muslim communities managed to maintain their identity and culture throughout Islamic history. This does not mean that there were no occasional discriminatory practices against non-Muslims, especially when evaluated from the perspective of modern human rights standards. However, although it may seem inadequate by today's standards compared to other societies, the degree of religious freedom provided by Muslim states throughout the Middle Ages was remarkably progressive. Also, Islamic law gave non-Muslim communities considerable autonomy and free will regarding internal issues related to education, tax collection, law, and religion, in addition to being exempted from military and government service. They could also establish and administer places of worship, courts, and religious foundations.

With regard to minorities, Andalusia is often seen as the basic example of a libertarian approach to Islamic law. Andalusia is not an exception, but an extension of Islamic practices elsewhere in the world.

For example, the roots of the Ottoman *millet* system can be traced back to the Covenant of Medina accepted by religious community leaders in the time of the Prophet Muhammad ﷺ. The Rightly Guided Caliphs, Umayyads, Abbasids, and Mughals who came after the Prophet Muhammad ﷺ also contributed to the development of the system. Therefore, it would be a mistake to say that the millet system is an Ottoman invention.

The Ottoman Empire followed the tradition of the millet system. It started with Fatih Sultan Mehmet (d. 1481), who improved upon the Ottoman institutional structure by explicitly expressing the rights of non-Muslim communities in imperial edicts. These edicts were called *ahdnāme* and held the power of an international agreement because it was the decree of the sultan.

As mentioned in some recent studies, Greek Orthodox Christians were not accepted as a religious community for the first time after Fatih Sultan Mehmet conquered Istanbul. On the contrary, they had the same community rights during the Umayyads, Abbasids, Seljuq and Ottoman times before the conquest of Istanbul. The patriarch was allowed to implement orthodox law with regard to communal and religious matters.

As the policy of religious pluralism and multiculturalism was reinforced by the *millet* system, it allowed Jews to establish their own communities and establish independent synagogues, schools for education, and courts in Istanbul.

Historians generally note that the freedom granted to minorities within Ottoman lands attracted displaced Jewish communities, who were victims of oppression in Spain, Poland, Austria, and Bohemia. The Jews who settled in the Muslim territories benefited greatly from remarkable tolerance and justice, unlike the oppression in Russia, Romania, and the Balkan states.[8]

Armenians were another major religious community that constituted a recognized millet under Ottoman rule. Sultan Mehmed the Conqueror (*Fatih Sultan Mehmed*) issued an imperial decree (*ahdnāme*) that officially entrusted the leadership of the Armenian Patriarchate to Hovakim, the newly appointed Patriarch of Istanbul. This formal recognition facilitated the organization of the Armenian community under its own religious and administrative authority. As a result, large numbers of Armenians migrated to Istanbul from regions such as Iran, the Caucasus, Eastern and Central Anatolia, the Balkans, and Crimea, which consolidated the city's position as a center of Armenian religious and cultural life within the empire.

This migration was not driven by oppression or forced displacement, but rather by the favorable conditions created under Ottoman governance during Fatih Sultan Mehmed's reign. The empire had become a genuine hub of Armenian life, where the community prospered. Until the eventual dissolution of the millet system and the onset of the Armenian Revolt, Armenians continued to expand and flourish within the Ottoman order.

In 1463, Fatih Sultan Mehmet also issued a declaration and edict of rights to the Bosnian Franciscans. Significant protections were similarly granted to the Catholic Church in Bosnia. Anđeo Zvizdović, the Franciscan representative, remained a "loyal servant of the Sultan, obedient to his sovereignty," as he promised in the edict, until he died in 1498.[9]

These declarations should be viewed as an acknowledgment of existing rights rather than declaring new rights not previously found in Islamic law. In fact, issuing such edicts was a custom of Muslim conquerors. It is widely known that after Jerusalem came under Muslim rule in 632, Caliph Umar issued an edict with similar content.[10]

The *millet* system can be seen as the main reason why the Ottoman Empire flourished for such an extended period of time. The system gave communities the right to self-governance, put local rulers in power and gave them many administrative responsibilities. Representatives of the *millets* were responsible for addressing many issues within their own religious communities rather than dealing directly with Ottoman officials. Chosen by members of their own communities, the role of religious leaders was to establish and maintain relations with the state. These leaders served as bridges between the government and their respective communities and ultimately served as intermediaries between the state and society. Different community groups acted on their own, independent of the state, as they had the power to organize their own legal, educational, and religious affairs.[11]

Within the *millet* system, managing relations between different religious communities posed significant challenges, particularly as inter-communal issues were more likely to give rise to legal and social tensions. One such issue was the admissibility of a witness from one religious community testifying against a defendant from another. Some jurists rejected such testimonies because of their concerns over potential bias that might arise from the religious differences between the suspect and the witness. Others, however, argued that religious difference in itself did not invalidate a person's capacity to bear witness, especially when supported by broader considerations of justice and procedural necessity.

Another sensitive matter was interreligious marriage. According to Islamic law, Muslim men were permitted to marry women from the People of the Book (*Ahl al-Kitāb*), while Muslim women were not allowed to marry non-Muslim men. This restriction was grounded in concerns about guardianship, religious continuity, and familial authority. Non-Muslim communities, for their part, prohibited interfaith marriages entirely within their own legal frameworks.

In terms of public identity, members of different millets were required to visibly display symbols of their religious affiliation, such as distinctive clothing or badges. This served not only to maintain communal boundaries and social roles but also functioned as a form of religious expression. However, with the advent of modernity and the rise of secular nation-states, such practices came to be seen as outdated and discriminatory. As secular identities increasingly supplanted religious ones in the public sphere, these markers of faith lost their normative place in social organization.

From a modern perspective, one of the most significant limitations of the *millet* system lies in the restriction that non-Muslims could not hold the highest political office, known in classical Islamic law as *al-wilāyah al-ʿāmmah* (general leadership). While non-Muslims were permitted to serve in various administrative capacities, including as ministers (*wuzarāʾ*) or advisors, they were not eligible to assume the role of head of state. This restriction also extended to Muslim women, based on the prevailing juristic consensus that the position of supreme political authority requires a Muslim male. Although legal interpretations vary across contemporary Muslim societies, this classical ruling continues to influence constitutional norms in some modern Islamic states.

Notes

1. Murat Şen, "The Historical Development of Turkish Law," *Hufs Global Law Review* 6, no. 2 (2014): 65-76.
2. Richard Bulliet, *The Case for Islamo-Christian Civilization* (Columbia University Press, 2004).
3. See Recep Şentürk, "Unity in Multiplexity: Islam as an Open Civilization," *Journal of the Interdisciplinary Study of Monotheistic Religions* 7 (2011): 49-60.
4. See Mahdi Zahraa, "Legal personality in Islamic law," *Arab Law Quarterly* 10 (1995): 193-206.
5. *Saḥiḥ Muslim* 1716a,Book 30, *Ḥadīth* 18.
6. Recep Şentürk, "Unity in Multiplexity: Islam as an Open Civilization."
7. The *Miḥnah* was an inquisition imposed by the Abbasid caliph al-Maʾmūn (833–848 CE) to enforce the Muʿtazilite doctrine that the Qur'an was created, rather than eternal. Scholars who refused to accept this view, like Aḥmad ibn Ḥanbal, were persecuted, imprisoned, or tortured. The *Miḥnah* ended when caliph al-Mutawakkil reversed the policy, reaffirming the traditional belief that the Qur'an was uncreated.
8. See Paul Dumont, "Jewish Communities in Turkey during the Last Decades of the Nineteenth Century in the Light of the Archives of the Alliance Israelite Universelle," in *Christians and Jews in the Ottoman Empire*, Vol. 1, eds. Benjamin Braude and Bernhard Lewis (New York: Holmes & Meier Publishers, 1982), 209-242.
9. Anđeo Zvizdović (1420-1498) was a Franciscan friar from Vrhbosna (modern-day Sarajevo), who played an essential role in the negotiations of the *Ahdnāme* of Milodraž with Fatih Sultan Mehmet, after the Ottoman conquest of Bosnia.
10. See Ibrahim Mohamed Zein and Ahmed El-Wakil, *The Covenants of the Prophet Muḥammad: From Shared Historical Memory to Peaceful Co-Existence*. Routledge, 2022.
11. See İlber Ortaylı, "Osmanlı İmparatorluğu'nda Millet," *Tanzimat'tan Cumhuriyete Türkiye Ansiklopedisi*, Vol. 4, Editor (PLACE: İletişim Yayınları, 1985), 996-1001. Also see Cevdet Küçük, "Osmanlılar'da 'Millet Sistemi' ve Tanzimat", in the same volume, 1007-1024.

CHAPTER SIX

From *Dhimmī* to Citizen: The Transition From the *Millet* System to the Nation-State

As the Muslim polity underwent processes of modernization, and secular conceptions of identity began to dominate, religious minorities were increasingly redefined in terms of ethnicity rather than religion, particularly within the context of the Ottoman Empire.[1] Under classical Islamic governance, the category of "minority" primarily referred to non-Muslims (*dhimmīs*), and the question of their legal, human, and constitutional rights was a major point of legal discussion, as noted in earlier chapters. However, with the gradual dissolution of the *millet* system, religious distinctions lost their legal salience and were supplanted by ethnic differentiations as the primary markers of identity.

The *millet* system had historically served to minimize ethnic tensions by organizing communities along confessional rather than ethnic lines. Yet by the nineteenth century, and especially after the weakening and eventual dismantling of the *millet* structure, ethnic identity began to emerge as a powerful social and political force. This shift coincided with the spread of European-style nationalism across the Islamic world, which contributed to a heightened sense of ethnic self-consciousness among various communities. As a result, many ethnic groups began to articulate broader claims, ranging from demands for expanded rights to aspirations for full independence.

In response to these transformations, the Ottoman state initiated a series of reforms aimed at redefining the basis of political belonging. These reforms culminated in the extension of equal citizenship rights to both Muslim and non-Muslim subjects, which marked a significant departure from the older system of differentiated legal status. The transition from *dhimmī* to citizen thus reflected not only a change in legal categories but also a broader reconfiguration of identity, governance, and the relationship between religion and the state.

In this context, the Gülhane Edict was issued in 1839 during the Tanzimat reforms. This declaration, which could be described as the first human rights declaration made by a Muslim state, guaranteed fundamental rights to all citizens. The Gülhane Edict of the Tanzimat was based on the teachings of inviolability (*ʿiṣmah*) in Islamic law. This edict is especially important because it confirms that Christians and Muslims have equal rights in education and government administration. The second stage of this reform process was the convening of the Ottoman Sultan's State Advisory Council (*Meclis-i Meşveret*) on March 24, 1855, to discuss how to reform the rights of minorities, especially Christians, in the empire. Reformist sultans and statesmen wanted to make the Ottoman state a modern European state.

This request, coupled with internal pressures from minorities and external pressures from European allies and enemies, instigated reforms in the practice of Islamic law. The council submitted the decisions to the consideration and approval of *Shaykh al-Islām* and received approval. On March 26, 1855, the council convened once again and put forward the most important official document on minority rights in Islamic law.

Islamic legitimacy for these reforms was drawn from the book *Kitāb al-Siyar al-Kabīr* of Muḥammad al-Shaybānī, the distinguished student of Abū Ḥanīfa.[2] Ottoman scholars and statesmen who sought to reform the legal system from a universalist perspective rediscovered in this text the foundational principles of a universalist strand within Islamic jurisprudence. By appealing to this authoritative text, they were able to confer religious legitimacy on the reform agenda, thereby securing broader acceptance among the ʿulamāʾ and the wider Muslim public. On February 18, 1856, these initiatives were formally proclaimed to the world through the *Islahat Fermanı* (Royal Decree of Reforms), which functioned as a declaration of rights and marked a pivotal moment in the Ottoman Empire's engagement with the global discourse on human rights.

The promulgation of the Ottoman constitution in 1876 marked the first formal step toward modern legal administration within the empire. It initiated the First Constitutional Era under Sultan Abdulhamid II, although this period lasted only about a year. For the first time, a parliamentary system was officially recognized, albeit with limited enforcement power and constrained political autonomy. The constitution included provisions concerning fundamental rights and liberties, judicial independence, and the security of judges. In 1909, the Young Turks deposed Abdulhamid II and ushered in the Second Constitutional Era, further institutionalizing the parliamentary system and laying the groundwork for the final phase of Ottoman constitutionalism before the empire's dissolution.[3]

From the Millet System to the Nation-State

The declaration of the constitutional system meant the abolition of the traditional *millet* system and the introduction of the modern nation-state model into the Ottoman Empire.[4] Since the *dhimmīs* at the individual level became equal citizens, it was no longer necessary to maintain separate communities under the leadership of religious leaders based on their religious and cultural identities.

As a result, the identities of major religious groups, such as Jews, Greeks, Armenians, Catholics, and Orthodox Christians, were redefined under a new collective designation: the "Ottoman nation." The term *millet*, which had historically signified a religious community, was secularized and reinterpreted to denote a political nation. However, the project of forging a unified national identity that encompassed all religious communities ultimately failed. In its place, ethnic groups began to assert themselves as minorities with distinct secular identities. Because Islamic law is premised on a religious rather than ethnic basis for communal organization, the Ottoman Empire, built on Islamic principles, lacked the ideological and legal tools to fully accommodate the rise of secular ethnic nationalism.[5]

The shift from a religiously defined social order to one based on secular-ethnic categories was neither smooth nor without consequence. Armenians, like all other minorities, can be regarded as victims of the collapse of the *millet* system, under which they had a safe and secure life with their Muslim neighbors for centuries. As ethnic identity gained political primacy, secular leadership within these communities rose in prominence. Many such leaders, particularly in Anatolia and the Balkans, sought autonomy or outright independence from the Ottoman state.

The disintegration of the empire eventually gave rise to a patchwork of new nation-states, governed either by secular or religious nationalist regimes. Within these emerging states, ethnic communities, once autonomous religious *millets*, were reclassified as minorities within a dominant national framework. In many Muslim-majority nation-states, the cultural and linguistic rights of ethnic minorities were often suppressed in the name of preserving national unity, which resulted in tensions between inherited religious models of coexistence and the homogenizing imperatives of modern nationalism.

Outside observers who are not familiar with the cultural dynamics of the Islamic world may erroneously attribute the practices of nationalist secular regimes in Muslim countries to Islamic law. In reality, the secularization of legal systems in many such states marks a significant rupture from the principles and structures of classical Islamic jurisprudence. Türkiye serves as a particularly illustrative example: a Muslim-majority country where the implementation of a secular legal order curtailed many of the protections and freedoms religious minorities had previously enjoyed under the Ottoman *millet* system.

The shift to secular governance did not automatically resolve long-standing issues related to minority rights. While some grievances were addressed, new challenges arose. Under the Ottoman Empire, the Kurds, an ethnically distinct Muslim population, were allowed to use their language freely, maintain their cultural traditions, and in many cases were entrusted with administrative and military responsibilities in their regions. However, the emergence of Turkish nationalism in the Republican era introduced assimilationist policies that marginalized Kurdish identity and imposed limitations on their cultural and linguistic expression.

Religious minorities also faced problems they did not experience under Ottoman rule, especially in the field of religious education, as the state centralized and nationalized religious institutions. The Republic of Türkiye abolished independent religious schools, banned Sufi orders, and placed tight controls on Christian missionary activities, none of which had been standard policy under Ottoman rule.

One of the most visible symbols of secularist intervention in religious life was the prohibition of the headscarf for Muslim women in public institutions. In the 1980s, students, civil servants, and even university professors were barred from wearing the headscarf. Similarly, the public display of religious piety among men, such as growing a beard, was also restricted for those employed in education or government service.

These transformations reflect the sharp contrast between the pluralistic, religiously-informed framework of the Ottoman-Islamic tradition and the homogenizing, top-down secularism that came to define the political landscape of the 20th century. Nevertheless, after more than a decade of legal battles, civil unrest, and sustained public resistance, the bans on religious expression, such as the headscarf and beards, were eventually lifted.

While countries like Türkiye moved away from religious legal traditions under the banner of secular nationalism, other post-Ottoman and postcolonial Muslim-majority states took a different path. Following the fall of the Ottoman Empire, some newly established states, such as Saudi Arabia, announced their intention to apply Islamic law.

Later in the twentieth century, countries like Pakistan, Iran, Sudan, Afghanistan, and Nigeria also joined this trend, formally declaring *sharīʿah* as the basis of their legal systems. However, the implementation of Islamic law in these contexts often departed significantly from the ethical and legal norms historically upheld by the Ottoman Empire or other traditional Islamic states. In particular, the treatment of minorities and the excessive application of capital punishment drew criticism from both Muslims and non-Muslims. These modern Islamic states did not adopt the universalist Islamic tradition grounded in the concept of *ādamiyyah*.

Instead, they tended to adopt the most restrictive interpretations, or outright misinterpretations, of Islamic law. As a result, the concept of *ādamiyyah*, representing universal humanity and the foundation of human dignity in Islamic law, has been largely neglected in the modern Muslim world. Its vision of equality and human dignity has yet to be meaningfully revived in most contemporary Muslim legal systems.

Notes

1. Muhittin Ataman, "Islamic Perspectives on Ethnicity and Nationalism: Diversity or Unity?" *Journal of Muslim Minority Affairs* 23, no. 1 (2003): 89-120.
2. Muḥammad b. al-Ḥasan al-Shaybānī, *Kitāb al-Siyar wa al-Kharāj wa al-ʿUshr min Kitāb al-Aṣl al-maʿrūf bi al-Mabsūṭ*, ed. Majid Khadduri (Karachi, 1996)
3. For the intellectual and political history of this period, see Şerif Mardin, *The Genesis of Young Ottoman Thought* (New Jersey: Princeton University Press, 1962); M. Şükrü Hanioğlu, *The Young Turks in Opposition* (New York and Oxford: Oxford University Press, 1995).
4. For a compilation of the Ottoman and Turkish constitutions, see Suna Kili and A. Şeref Gözübüyük, *Türk Anayasa Metinleri* (Istanbul: Türkiye İş Bankası Yayınları, 1985).
5. For a study on the final years of the nineteenth-century Ottoman reforms, see Ali Akyıldız, *Osmanlı Bürokrasisi ve Modernleşme* (Istanbul: İletişim Yayınları, 2004).

CHAPTER SEVEN

I Am Therefore I Have Duties

Our existence as human beings forms the foundation not only for our rights but also for our responsibilities. Just as our humanity entitles us to certain rights, it also imposes upon us corresponding duties. There is a symmetrical relationship between rights and duties: the rights of others are our duties. Duties, in turn, are the price we pay to enjoy our rights. While much discourse has been devoted to the universality of rights as a fundamental aspect of our existence, it is equally imperative to acknowledge universal duties, which stem from the same ontological ground, our humanity (*ādamiyyah*).

The concept of *ādamiyyah* is not only the source of our rights but also the source of our obligations. By virtue of being created as human beings, we are designated as vicegerents (*khulafāʾ*) of Allah on earth. This divine appointment is explicitly stated in the Qur'an: "*Behold, your Lord said to the angels: 'I will create a vicegerent on earth.*'" (Qur'an, 2:30) Thus, human beings who have been entrusted with the moral and ethical governance of the world bear an inherent responsibility towards all of creation to serve as stewards.

The role of *khalīfah* entails not only representation but also the fulfillment of divine will through divinely mandated responsibilities that are entrusted to human beings as *amānah* (the duty of divine stewardship). Allah has endowed humans with reason, free will, and fundamental rights, including the rights to life, freedom, and property, not as ends in themselves, but as means to fulfill our obligations. The superior qualities bestowed upon human beings are intended to enable them to uphold their duties toward Allah, fellow human beings, and all of creation, as al-Sarakhsī and ʿAbd al-ʿAzīz al-Bukhārī articulate in their jurisprudential works.

This understanding of human agency and responsibility also corresponds to a broader vision of the purposes of Islamic law, which seeks not only to regulate individual conduct but to sustain the moral and social order. In this regard, Ibn ʿĀshūr, in his *Maqāṣid al-Sharīʿah al-Islāmiyyah*, states that the overarching purpose of Islamic law is not only to secure individual benefits but to preserve the order and well-being of the community through the well-being of the human being. The well-being of humans, he argues, consists of three essential dimensions: the soundness of human intellect, the righteousness of human action, and the proper management of the resources of the world in which humans live.[1] Thus, rights and duties are inseparable: the rights of each person are upheld through the responsibilities of others, and the duties each person bears are essential to ensuring the rights and well-being of all.

The Ultimate Purpose of *Sharīʿah*: Preserving Social Order and Human Well-being

Ibn ʿĀshūr (d. 1973), *Maqāṣid al-Sharīʿah al-Islāmiyyah**

إذا نحن استقرينا مواردَ الشريعةِ الإسلاميةِ الدالة على مقاصِدها من التشريع، استبانَ لنا من كليات دلائلها ومن جزئياتها المستقرأةِ أنَّ المقصدَ العام من التشريع فيها هو حفظُ نظامِ الأمة واستدامةُ صلاحِه بصلاحِ المهيمن عليه، وهو نوعُ الإنسان. ويشمل صلاحُه صلاحَ عقله، وصلاحَ عملِه، وصلاحَ ما بين يديه من موجودات العالم الذي يعيش فيه.

If we examine the sources of Islamic law that indicate its higher objectives (*maqāṣid*) in legislation, it becomes clear to us, through both its general principles and its specific rulings, that the overarching purpose of legislation in Islam is to preserve the order of the community and to ensure its continued well-being by ensuring the well-being of those entrusted to its care, namely, the human being. The well-being of humans encompasses the well-being of human intellect, human action, and the resources of the world in which humans live.

*Muḥammad al-Ṭāhir ibn ʿĀshūr, *Maqāṣid al-Sharīʿah al-Islāmiyyah* (Amman: Dār al-Nafāʾis, 2001), 273.

The basic universal duty that originates from *ādamiyyah* is to fulfill *ḥuqūq Allāh* (the rights of God) and *ḥuqūq al-ʿibād* (the rights of human beings). In Islamic legal tradition, rights are broadly categorized into these two domains, with some scholars also recognizing a third category that encompasses rights that commonly belong both to God and human beings. Observing *ḥuqūqullāh* is described as *taʿẓīm li-amrillāh* (showing reverence for God's command) while fulfilling *ḥuqūq al-ʿibād* is described as *al-shafaqah ʿalā khalqillāh* (showing compassion toward God's creation).

Ḥuqūq Allāh refers to the rights of God, in other words, the duties that human beings owe to Him. These include obligations that directly pertain to one's relationship with Allah, such as acts of worship (*ʿibādāt*). Beyond the individual acts of worship, *ḥuqūq Allāh* also extends to obligations that prevent corruption and uphold social order, justice, and the well-being of the community. Among these obligations are the implementation of punishments (*ḥudūd*) for major offenses such as theft, adultery, and false accusation, as well as other social responsibilities such as ensuring access to public resources like roads, waterways, and places of worship.

On the other hand, *ḥuqūq al-ʿibād* pertains to the rights and responsibilities one holds in relation to fellow human beings. These include fundamental rights such as the protection of life, dignity, property, and family. Violations of these rights, such as unjustly harming others, committing theft, slander, fraud, or oppression, constitute an infringement upon *ḥuqūq al-ʿibād* and are considered acts of injustice.

Unlike *ḥuqūq Allāh*, which lies solely within God's discretion to pardon, transgressions against *ḥuqūq al-ʿibād* require direct restitution and reparation. One cannot simply seek divine forgiveness for violating another's rights without rectifying the harm done. Ibn al-Najjār al-Ḥanbalī (d. 1564) articulates this principle succinctly: "*Ḥaqq Allāh yazūlu bi al-tawbah, wa ḥaqq al-ādamī yazūlu bi zawāl athar al-ẓulm*" (violation of the divine rights disappears with repentance, but the violation of human rights disappears only with the removal of the impact of injustice).[2] Thus, justice is not fulfilled through remorse but through the restoration of the rights of the wronged party.

Moreover, *ḥuqūq al-ʿibād* assumes even greater significance when it comes to those who are unable to defend their own rights, such as orphans, widows, the impoverished, and marginalized groups. Islam insists upon the protection of these vulnerable members of society and warns that any neglect or exploitation of their rights is a grave injustice that incurs divine punishment.

The seriousness of violating *ḥuqūq al-ʿibād* is expressed by Abū al-ʿAbbās al-Wansharīsī (d. 1509), who states that "*balad fīhi maʿāṣin fī ḥuqūq Allāh taʿālā fa huwa awlā min balad fīhi maʿāṣin fī maẓālim al-ʿibād*" (a land in which the rights of God are violated is preferred over a land in which humans are violated in their rights).[3] While neglecting God's rights is a grave sin, it still falls within God's vast mercy and forgiveness. But violating human rights, whether through oppression, economic injustice, or social exploitation, causes harm that repentance alone cannot undo. Thus, standing up for the rights of others is a core part of fulfilling our duties before God.

This connection between the rights of others and our ultimate accountability is made even clearer in the well-known narration of the Prophet Muhammad ﷺ. He once asked his companions, "Do you know who the bankrupt is?" They replied, "O Messenger of Allah! The bankrupt among us is the one who has no money or property." But the Prophet ﷺ corrected them, saying:

> "The bankrupt in my ummah is the one who comes on the Day of Judgement with prayer, fasting, and charity, but he comes having abused this person, falsely accused that person, unlawfully consumed another's wealth, shed someone's blood, and beaten another person. As a result, his good deeds will be taken and distributed among those he wronged. If his good deeds run out, the sins of those he oppressed will be transferred to him, and he will be thrown into the Hellfire."[4]

In this narration, the Prophet ﷺ teaches us that our duties to other human beings are inseparable from our relationship with God. People may fulfill their obligations to Allah through prayer, fasting, and charity but if they violate the rights of others, all those acts of worship cannot save them from divine justice.

Yet, when it comes to our responsibility to uphold justice and prevent harm, scholars have long debated the scope and limits of this duty. Broadly speaking, we can identify two perspectives on this issue: the *ādamiyyah* perspective and the *ibrāhīmiyyah* perspective. From the *ādamiyyah* perspective, it is our obligation to oppose any form of injustice wherever it occurs, and whoever the victim may be. Under this view, the duty to defend human rights is universal. Every Muslim whether as an individual or as part of a governing body, is responsible for standing against oppression and working to restore justice. To remain silent in the face of injustice is itself an act of injustice.

On the other hand, the *ibrāhīmiyyah* perspective also affirms the necessity of justice yet places a different emphasis on jurisdiction and responsibility. It argues that the first and foremost duty is to respect the rights of all, without violating or oppressing anyone. When it comes to actively enforcing justice and intervening, this duty applies specifically within the scope of one's legal and political authority, that is, within the Islamic polity and jurisdiction. From this standpoint, while Muslims must respect the rights of non-citizens and outsiders, their primary duty of enforcement is limited to their own community, where they hold legal power and responsibility.

Do Rights Depend on Duties?

Another major distinction between the *ādamiyyah* and *ibrāhimiyyah* paradigms lies in how they conceive the relationship between rights and duties. From the *ādamiyyah* perspective, universal rights are inherent and inalienable. They are granted directly by God to every human being simply by virtue of being *ādamī* (a member of the human family). These rights are intrinsic to human dignity and do not depend on whether or not we fulfill our duties.

In this view, even when a person neglects their moral or legal obligations, they do not lose their essential rights, such as the right to life, dignity, and protection. Though they may be held accountable and punished for failing in their responsibilities, their fundamental rights continue to belong to them by virtue of their *ādamiyyah,* their status as human beings created and honored by God.

On the other hand, the *ibrāhimiyyah* perspective takes a different approach, arguing that rights are tied to duties. From this viewpoint, rights are not granted by default. They depend on a person's willingness to fulfill their responsibilities. If a person neglects those responsibilities, some rights may no longer apply.

For example, in this framework, someone who refuses to pay the *jizyah,* a tax that guarantees non-Muslim citizens protection and recognition within the state, can lose their right to *ʿiṣmah*, or legal inviolability. The idea here is clear: a person cannot claim the benefits of living in a community without also carrying their share of its responsibilities and burdens. In other words, protection is conditional on contributing to the system that maintains everyone's safety and order.

Classification of Duties: Legal and Moral

Just as rights can be divided into legal or moral categories, duties are also classified into two major types: legal duties (*wājibāt sharʿiyyah*) and moral duties (*wājibāt akhlāqiyyah*). Legal duties are obligations that are enforceable by law, such as respecting life, property, and dignity. Examples include the duty not to harm others, not to steal, and to fulfill contractual obligations. These duties are backed by legal mechanisms, meaning the state or governing authority has the right to compel individuals to fulfill them or punish violations. Without adherence to legal duties, the basic fabric of society would collapse.

Moral duties, on the other hand, are obligations that stem from ethics and conscience. They represent what a person ought to do from a moral and humane perspective, even if there is no legal enforcement. Examples include showing compassion, helping those in need, being honest, and forgiving others. These duties are about the higher values that sustain trust, mercy, and solidarity within a community. While legal duties are essential for maintaining order and protecting basic rights, moral duties are what give society its soul. This is where the distinction between law and morality becomes clear. Law is based on justice, whereas morality is based on love.

Yet in modern philosophical debates, justice has been widely upheld as the supreme principle for organizing society. Leading thinkers such as John Rawls, Robert Nozick, Michael Sandel, Thomas Pogge, and Michael Boylan have long debated what justice means and how to realize it in social and political life. For many, justice has become the highest ideal, though even among these scholars, there is a recognition that achieving perfect justice may be more of an aspiration than a reality.

However, in the Islamic worldview, justice is not the highest organizing principle. Rather, it is seen as the minimum necessity for a good society that could be achieved through the implementation of divine law, the *Sharīʿah*. Love, on the other hand, is viewed as the highest organizing principle and an ideal for society. This idea is eloquently articulated by Kınalızâde Ali Efendi (1510–1572), a renowned Ottoman jurist and moral philosopher, in his influential work *Ahlâk-ı Alâî*. He writes:

"It has become apparent that humans need to live together and interact with each other in order to achieve order in their lives and attain happiness and perfection. However, living together and interacting with others also leads to conflicts and opposition. There are two ways to prevent this: The first is the path of **justice** and the establishment of laws of governance. This path is for the general public and includes all classes and groups of society. The second way is the path of **love**, which is attainable only by the elite (*khawāṣ*) and the distinguished (*aʿyān*), for it is nearly impossible for the majority of people to genuinely love one another. When a society adheres to the path of love, there is no need for the path of justice. Justice becomes necessary because individuals pursue their own desires, and the collision of competing claims gives rise to disputes. From the pursuit of self-interest, contention is born. In contrast, love is characterized by altruism (*īthār*) where a person gives up something for the beloved and even desires it more for the beloved than for themselves.

Philosophers say that **love is superior to justice**. Love represents a natural unity, whereas justice reflects an artificial unity. Beware that natural should not be like artificial! Love entails unity and dissolves duality. Justice, by contrast, arises after the realization of duality for justice is *inṣāf* (the moral sense of giving the other their due with fairness), and *inṣāf* is derived from the word 'half ' (*niṣf*), which means taking one half for oneself and giving the other half to the other. Sharing halves occurs when there is duality.

But when unity is realized through love, what need remains for the rules of duality? What benefit can they bring? As the wise have said:

The well-being and continuity of all things depend on love."[5]

In this vision, love is not only an individual virtue but the highest organizing principle of society. If justice is about ensuring that everyone gets their fair share, love calls us to go beyond fairness: to give more than what is due and to care for others as we would for ourselves, if not more. This is also the heart of *futuwwah* ethics derived from the Qur'an and the Sunnah of the Prophet Muhammad ﷺ which encourages treating others with a higher standard of generosity, kindness, and sacrifice.[6]

Is There a Right to Sin or Crime?

The inviolability of human beings does not grant them unrestricted freedom to act without moral or legal constraints. While every individual is entitled to protection and dignity, this does not mean they are free to do whatever they wish without accountability. Rights and duties exist in a symmetrical relationship: just as we claim rights, we must also fulfill corresponding obligations. A just society is not built solely on the recognition of rights but on the balance between rights and responsibilities, which applies at both the communal and global levels.

Thus, the universalist *ādamiyyah* paradigm, which affirms the inherent dignity and rights of every human being, does not imply that people are free to act without regard for ethical or normative boundaries. Rather, it situates human rights within a broader moral universe. Muslims, for instance, are expected to abide by the ethical and legal principles of Islam, while followers of other faiths are equally expected to observe the moral norms of their own religious traditions, especially in how they treat others.

Moreover, across religious and cultural divides, there are common moral principles referred to as global ethics that affirm the dignity of others and establish the basic norms for human interaction. These universal values operate alongside the particular norms unique to each religion and culture. These two levels create a multiplex framework of responsibility: some duties are universally binding upon all human beings, while others are specific to particular faith traditions or social contexts.

In conclusion, the inviolability of human beings does not entitle them to disregard the moral and social norms that define and regulate their relationships with others. Every individual is obligated to uphold these norms both at the global level and within their own communities. This is the meaning of the symmetry between rights and duties.

Notes

1. Muḥammad al-Ṭāhir ibn ʿĀshūr, *Maqāṣid al-Sharīʿah al-Islāmiyyah* (Amman: Dār al-Nafāʾis, 2001).
2. Abū al-Abbās al-Wansharīsī, *al-Miʿyār al-Muʿrib wa al-Jāmiʿ al-Mughrib ʿan Fatāwā Ahl Ifrīqiyyah wa al-Maghrib*, vol.2 (DKI: Dār al-Kutub al-ʿilmiyyah, 2011), 113.
3. Ibn al-Najjār al-Ḥanbalī, *Mukhtaṣar al-Taḥrīr* (DKI: Dār al-Kutub al-ʿilmiyyah, 2007), 113.
4. Jāmiʿ al-Tirmidhī 2418, Book 37, Ḥadīth 4.
5. Kınalızâde Ali. *Ahlâk-ı Alâî* (Istanbul: Klasik Yayınları, 2007), 418–420.
6. See my previous work on *futuwwah* ethics, Recep Şentürk, *Futuwwah: Noble Character* (Usul Academy, 2022).

CONCLUSION

Towards a New Vision for Rights and Duties

As this book has demonstrated, Islamic law upholds a universalist legal approach to rights and duties. Across the various schools of Islamic legal thought, there is consensus on the inherent dignity of all human beings, as affirmed in the Qur'anic conception of human sanctity and honor (*karāmah*). The divergence among jurists does not concern the existence of universal rights, but rather their enforceability: whether these rights must be upheld unconditionally across all contexts, or whether their implementation is contingent upon political and legal authority within an Islamic framework. This distinction is crucial for understanding the diversity of interpretations regarding human rights in Islamic law and their implications for contemporary legal and ethical discourse.

While similar concepts can be found in other religious and philosophical traditions, what distinguishes Islamic fiqh is that such principles are not merely rational deductions or moral ideals; they are codified within the framework of sharīʿah law. As a result, they are legally binding and subject to defined legal consequences for violation. The inviolability of every human being (*ʿiṣmah*) is thus not only a moral imperative but a legal obligation, upheld by the state and incumbent upon all Muslims. This creates a dual system of enforcement: one legal, through state authority, and the other spiritual, through individual faith and conscience. Moreover, Islamic belief affirms that those who evade justice in this world will ultimately be held accountable in the hereafter.

Islam also recognizes the existence of universal moral rights alongside legal rights. These moral rights are also grounded in the concept of *ādamiyyah*, the universal brotherhood of humanity. This moral vision is embodied in the principle of *futuwwah*, which emphasizes noble character, humility, and altruism, prioritizing the well-being of others over self-interest. While legal rights regulate external obligations and protections, moral rights encourage goodness within and bring people together. Together, these legal and moral dimensions shape the comprehensive nature of human rights in Islam.

This book has also engaged critically with the epistemological tensions between Eurocentric and universalist frameworks in the discourse on human rights. A central contention that emerges is the fallacy of attributing universality exclusively to Western intellectual traditions. This claim is mostly perpetuated by Eurocentric historiographies. The conceptualization of inborn and inalienable rights was not only present but foundational within the Islamic juridical tradition, particularly in the Ḥanafī school, where it informed legal reasoning and institutional practice across diverse Islamic polities. This robust legacy of Islamic rights discourse facilitated a receptive engagement with modern human rights language in many parts of the Muslim world, not as a novel imposition, but as a continuation and codification of principles long held to be intrinsic to the Islamic worldview. What is often framed as adoption is, in many cases, better understood as a process of discursive reaffirmation within contemporary international legal frameworks.[1]

Another key finding is the divergence in the epistemic and discursive frameworks through which universal human rights are conceptualized in Islamic and Western traditions. In the Islamic intellectual tradition, the articulation of human rights is embedded within the normative and jurisprudential corpus of classical *fiqh*, grounded in divine revelation and legal methodology. By contrast, in the Western context, human rights discourse emerged from Enlightenment-era political theory and secular legal philosophy. This disparity in conceptual genealogy has often resulted in misreadings, incommensurable categories, or superficial analogies that obscure the internal coherence and depth of each tradition. A sound comparative approach requires attending to the distinct ontological and epistemological commitments that undergird each framework.

Furthermore, it is analytically untenable to treat Islamic legal discourse as a monolithic entity, given its evolution over centuries through multiple jurisprudential schools, each with its own normative emphases. A rigorous comparative inquiry into human rights traditions thus necessitates an approach that is neither reductive nor dismissive, but one that critically engages the internal diversity of Islamic legal thought alongside its Western counterparts. Scholars working at the intersection of Islamic law and human rights must attend to this discursive multiplicity, rather than seeking coherence through artificial homogenization, if they are to produce analyses that faithfully reflect the depth of these intellectual traditions.

The *Ādamiyyah* paradigm, which represents a universalist conception of rights grounded in the foundational principle that "inviolability is due by virtue of humanity," was historically operationalized across Islamic civilizations. Yet today, no state formally enshrines this vision in its legal system, nor does any prevailing discourse within the Muslim world champion its revival. This absence is a profound loss, especially at a time when global human rights discourse is grappling with a deep crisis of legitimacy, marred by politicization, double standards, and selective enforcement. The eclipse of *ādamiyyah* is not only a departure from Islamic legal heritage but also a missed opportunity to offer a robust alternative to the fractured moral landscape of contemporary international law.

Now, more than ever, in our interconnected and globalized world, there is a pressing need for an ethical, legal, and political framework based on *ādamiyyah* that prioritizes justice, equality, and the sanctity of human life for all people. Reviving our social memory and reintroducing the idea of *ādamiyyah* to the entire world will bring a new incentive to the field of human rights, which is currently undergoing a crisis. The rich legacy of classical Islamic legal and ethical thought, preserved in centuries of *fiqh* literature, is waiting to be rediscovered and reinterpreted by a new generation of scholars.

Ādamiyyah offers a compelling conceptual, legal, and moral foundation for an *open civilization*: a pluralistic, justice-oriented social order that once characterized the Islamic world prior to its eclipse during the colonial period. The intellectual and political subjugation of the Muslim world disrupted this civilizational ethos. The intellectual independence of the Muslim mind and the rooted revival of the Islamic tradition are indispensable steps toward restoring this vision.

This call is not exclusive to Muslims. All followers of the Abrahamic traditions, and indeed all of humanity, are invited to renew their pledge to the universal covenant of Adam: a primordial moral commitment that affirms the dignity, unity, and inviolability of humankind before God. *Ādamiyyah* and the Adamic covenant once provided the ethical and legal foundation for human unity, recognition of human dignity, and a just social order. Central to this vision is a relational ethic of rights and duties, in which rights such as the preservation of life, intellect, faith, and property are inseparable from the responsibility to uphold them for others. The well-being of each individual is entrusted to the moral conscience and legal responsibility of the community. This covenantal vision offers a path forward, toward an open civilization held together by the recognition of the dignity and inviolability of every human being.

Notes

1. See for example Hüseyin Kâzim Kadri, *İnsan Hakları Beyannamesi'nin İslâm Hukukuna Göre İzahı* (Istanbul: ed. Osman Ergin, 1949), 43-87.

Bibliography

Abdel Haleem, M. H. S. *The Qur'an*. New York: Oxford University Press, 2010.

Akyıldız, Ali. *Osmanlı Bürokrasisi ve Modernleşme*. Istanbul: İletişim Yayınları, 2004.

Ali, Kecia. "Marriage in Classical Islamic Jurisprudence: A Survey of Doctrines." in *The Islamic Marriage Contract: Case Studies in Islamic Family Law*, edited by Asifa Qurayshi and Frank E. Vogel. Cambridge, MA and London: Harvard University Press, 2009.

Al-ʿAyni, Badr al-Din. *Al-Bināya fī Sharḥ al-Hidāya*. Edited by Muhammad Omar. Beirut: Dār al-Fikr, 1980/1400.

Arnold, Thomas W. *The Preaching of Islam: A History of the Propagation of the Muslim Faith*, 2nd ed. London: Constable & Company, 1913.

Ataman, Muhittin. "Islamic Perspectives on Ethnicity and Nationalism: Diversity or Unity?" *Journal of Muslim Minority Affairs* 23, no. 1 (2003): 89-120.

Ayoub, Samy. "The Mecelle, Sharia, and the Ottoman State: Fashioning and Refashioning of Islamic Law in the Nineteenth and Twentieth Centuries." *Journal of the Ottoman and Turkish Studies Association* 2, no. 1 (2015): 121-146.

Azzam, Salem. "Universal Declaration of Islamic Human Rights." *The International Journal of Human Rights* 2, no. 3 (1998): 102-112.

Braude, Benjamin, and Bernard Lewis, eds. *Christians and Jews in the Ottoman Empire: The Functioning of a Plural Society*. 2 vols. New York: Holmes & Meier, 1982.

Al-Bukhari, ʿAbdulaziz. *Kashf al-Asrār ʿan Uṣūl Fakhr al-Islām al-Bazdawī*. Edited by Muhammad al-Muʿtaṣim billah al-Baghdadi. Beirut: Dār al-Kitāb al-ʿArabī, 1418/1997.

Bulliet, Richard. *The Case for Islamo-Christian Civilization*. Columbia University Press, 2004.

Dembour, Marie-Bénédicte. "What Are Human Rights? Four Schools of Thought." *Human Rights Quarterly* 32, no. 1 (2010): 1-20.

Dumont, Paul. "Jewish Communities in Turkey during the Last Decades of the Nineteenth Century in the Light of the Archives of the Alliance Israelite Universelle." In *Christians and Jews in the Ottoman Empire*, vol. 1, edited by Benjamin Braude and Bernard Lewis. New York: Holmes & Meier Publishers, 1982.

El Shamsy, Ahmed. *The Canonization of Islamic Law: A Social and Intellectual History*. New York: Cambridge University Press, 2013.

Al-Ghazālī, Abū Ḥāmid. *The Book of Knowledge*. Translated by Kenneth Honerkamp. Fons Vitae, 2016.

Hallaq, Wael B. *Islamic Legal Theories: An Introduction to Sunnī Uṣūl al-Fiqh*. Cambridge: Cambridge University Press, 1997.

Hallaq, Wael B. *Sharīʿa: Theory, Practice, Transformations*. New York: Cambridge University Press, 2009.

Hanioğlu, M. Şükrü. *The Young Turks in Opposition*. New York and Oxford: Oxford University Press, 1995.

Hannum, Hurst. "The Status of the Universal Declaration of Human Rights in National and International Law." *Georgia Journal of International and Comparative Law* 25, no. 1-2 (1995): 289-397.

Ibn ʿĀbidīn, Muḥammad Amīn. *Radd al-Muḥtār ʿalā al-Durr al-Mukhtār*. Istanbul: Kahraman Yay, 1984.

Ivison, Duncan. *Rights*. Stocksfield: Acuman, 2008.

Al-Jayyusi, Salma al-Khadra, ed. *Ḥuqūq al-Insān fī al-Fikr al-ʿArabī*. Beirut: Markaz Dirāsāt al-Waḥda al-ʿArabiyya, 2002.

Johansen, Baber. *Contingency in a Sacred Law: Legal and Ethical Norms in the Muslim Fiqh*. Leiden: Brill, 1999.

Kadri, Hüseyin Kâzım. *İnsan Hakları Beyannamesi'nin İslâm Hukukuna Göre İzahı*. Istanbul: Osman Ergin, 1949.

Karamali, Hamza. *The Madrasa Curriculum in Context*. Abu Dhabi, UAE: Kalam Research and Media, 2017.

Al-Kāsānī, ʿAlāʾ al-Dīn. *Badāʾiʿ al-Ṣanāʾiʿ fī Tartīb al-Sharāʾiʿ*. Beirut: Dar al-Fikr, 1986.

Khadduri, Majid. *War and Peace in the Law of Islam*. Baltimore: The Johns Hopkins Press, 1955.

Kili, Suna, and A. Şeref Gözübüyük. *Türk Anayasa Metinleri*. Istanbul: Türkiye İş Bankası Yayınları, 1985.

Küçük, Cevdet. "Osmanlılar'da 'Millet Sistemi' ve Tanzimat." in *Tanzimat'tan Cumhuriyete Türkiye Ansiklopedisi*, vol. 4, edited by Murat Belge and Fahri Aral. Istanbul: İletişim Yayınları, 1985.

Makdisi, George. *The Rise of Colleges: Institutions of Learning in Islam and the West*. Edinburgh: Edinburgh University Press, 1981.

Mardin, Şerif. *The Genesis of Young Ottoman Thought*. New Jersey: Princeton University Press, 1962.

Al-Marghinānī, Burhān al-Dīn. *Al-Hidāyah: The Guidance*, vol. 1. Translated by Imran Ahsan Khan Nyazee. Bristol: Amal Press, 2006.

Al-Marghinānī, Burhān al-Dīn. *Al-Hidāyah fī Sharḥ Bidāyat al-Mubtadī*, vols. I-IV. Edited by Muhammad Tamir and Hafiz 'Ashur Hafiz. Cairo: Dar al-Salaam, 1420/2000.

Al-Maydānī, ʿAbd al-Ghanī. *Al-Lubāb fī Sharḥ al-Kitāb*. Edited by Muhammad Muhyiddin Abdulhamid. Cairo, 1383/1963.

Melchert, Christopher. *The Formation of the Sunni Schools of Law, 9th-10th Centuries C.E.* Leiden: Brill, 1997.

Mol, Arnold Yasin. "Islamic Human Rights Discourse and Hermeneutics of Continuity." *Journal of Islamic Ethics* 3, no. 1-2 (2019): 180-206.

Mubed, Zulfaqar. *Hinduism During the Mughal India of the 17th Century*. Translated by David Shea and Anthony Troyer. Patna: Khuda Bakhsh Oriental Public Library, 1993.

Ortaylı, İlber. "Osmanlı İmparatorluğu'nda Millet." in *Tanzimat'tan Cumhuriyete Türkiye Ansiklopedisi*, vol. 4, edited by Murat Belge and Fahri Aral. Istanbul: İletişim Yayınları, 1985.

O'Sullivan, Declan. "The Arab, European, Inter-American and African Perspectives on Understanding Human Rights: The Debate Between Universalism and Cultural Relativism." *Mediterranean Journal of Human Rights* 8, no. 1 (2004): 153-194.

O'Sullivan, Declan. "Is the Declaration of Human Rights Universal?" *The International Journal of Human Rights* 4, no. 1 (2000): 25-53.

Özel, Ahmet. *İslam Hukukunda Ülke Kavramı: Darûl İslam Darûl Harb*. Istanbul: İz Yayınları, 1998.

Sharawi, Tareq. "How Does Islam Treat People Outside the Abrahamic Religions? Between Ādamiyyah and Ibrāhimiyyah." PhD diss., Ibn Haldun University, 2020.

Sharawi, Tareq. "The Inviolability of the Non-Muslims in Islamic Law: A Comparative Reading of Modern and Classical Debates." *Afkār: Journal of 'Aqidah and Islamic Thought* 1 (2020): 79-112.

Sharma, Sri Ram. *The Religious Policy of the Mughal Emperors*. Una, Himachal Pradesh: Asia Publishing House, 1972.

Şen, Murat. "The Historical Development of Turkish Law." *Hufs Global Law Review* 6, no. 2 (2014): 65-76.

Şentürk, Recep. "Unity in Multiplexity: Islam as an Open Civilization." *Journal of the Interdisciplinary Study of Monotheistic Religions* 7 (2011): 49-60.

Şentürk, Recep, and Muhammed Said Bilal. *Human Rights in the Ottoman Reform: Foundations, Motivations and Formations*. Istanbul: İbn Haldun Üniversitesi Yayınları, 2020.

Şentürk, Recep. *Futuwwah: Noble Character*. Usul Academy, 2022.

Şentürk, Recep. *Semiotics of Nature: Recharging Nature with Meaning for Environmental Ethics and Action*. Doha: Hamad Bin Khalifa University Press, 2025.

Stroumsa, Guy G. *The Making of Abrahamic Religions in Late Antiquity*. New York: Oxford University Press, 2015.

Vlug, Jeroen. "The Contested Grounds of Human Rights in Islam and The West: A Comparative Study." PhD diss., Ibn Haldun University, 2023.

Vlug, Jeroen. "The Islamic Pursuit of Human Dignity: Revisiting Fundamental Rights Theories in Islamic Law and Legal Philosophy." *Cross-Cultural Human Rights Review* 2, no. 1 (2020): 23-48.

Wilson, Bryan. *Religion in Sociological Perspective*. Oxford and New York: Oxford University Press, 1982.

Zahraa, Mahdi. "Legal Personality in Islamic Law." *Arab Law Quarterly* 10 (1995): 193-206.

Al-Zamakhsharī. *Ru'ūs al-Masā'il al-Khilāfiyyah bayn al-Ḥanafiyyah wa al-Shāfi'īyyah*. Edited by Abdullah Nazır Ahmed. Diyarbakir: İslâmî Kitaplar Naşiri, n.d.

www.ingramcontent.com/pod-product-compliance
Lightning Source LLC
Chambersburg PA
CBHW030841270326
41928CB00007B/1162
9781965242025